TAGORE'S SONGS ON SOLIDARITY

TAGORE'S SONGS ON SOLIDARITY

MOHIT CHAKRABARTI

ABHIJEET PUBLICATIONS
DELHI 110094

ABHIJEET PUBLICATIONS
2/46 Tukhmeerpur Extension
Delhi-110 094
Phone: 011-22960492, 65698474
E-mail: abhijeetpublication@gmail.com

TAGORE'S SONGS ON SOLIDARITY

First Published 2008

ISBN 978-81-89886-59-2

PRINTED IN INDIA

Published by J.K. Singh for Abhijeet Publications, Delhi-110 094, Lasertypeset by Gaurav Graphics, New Delhi and Printed at Himanshu Printers, Delhi.

Dedicated to

Shri Rongomoy Chakrabarti

Preface

Solidarity is a human instinct, a typical design of behaviour and a way of manifestation of the self in terms of others and *vice versa*. To Rabindranath Tagore, it is more than that. It is, as he believes and translates in the incomparable language of inwardness, a continual striving for ascent and excellence of man. It cares more for an endless journey of the aesthetics for goodness and serenity, humility and poignancy. It crosses the narrow domestic or societal world of mere togetherness and refines human sensibilities in all forms of contemplation and action for ensuring the ends-in-view of fullness of man and beyond that.

Admittedly, Tagore's songs on solidarity present us with a panorama of humans in terms of self-realisation that welcomes the fundamental components of the excellence of the individual e.g. soul-consciousness, love, freedom, hope, beauty, joy, bereavement, patriotism, prayer and fusion with the Infinite. What prompts one in delving deep into these songs on solidarity may be spelt out from fivefold avenue of self-crystallisation. First, in the very concept of solidarity, Tagore has broadened the canvas of unity for global solidarity and so his songs on solidarity are extended a warm and heartening welcome by one and all irrespective of caste, creed, nationality, colour, clime, community or conformity to any kind of ideology. That these songs are endeared and honoured in an incomparable and unparalleled manner can be readily assessed and proved by the fact that his two ever prominent songs on solidarity are the national songs of Bangladesh and India. What a prize and glory for his songs on solidarity! Second, Tagore breaks all barriers of narrowness through his vision of vastness, elimination of the self and glory of the great 'We' in togetherness. Third, his vision on the integration of emotion and sensibilities coupled with finer feelings of joy, hope, loneliness, love and devotion paves an altogether newer avenue of self-identity in terms of solidarity. Fourth, as every human being is subject to sentimentalism, Tagore makes a significant departure from the ordinary platform of askance and enquiry and, instead, allows ample room for the solidarity of soul-consciousness. This component finds its aura of poignancy amidst a canvas of purity and simplicity in thought and expression. Fifth, the songs on solidarity also accelerate the vision of spirituality where Tagore is at his best in designing and exploring newer avenues of inwardness through realisation of the Infinite.

The songs on solidarity presented here prepare us to date with humanity that looks forward to ascent and excellence. Somewhere in every one of us there is an ever lingering and penetrating anguish for the finest forms of the All Serene which Tagore refers to as *Jeevandevata,* the God of Life, eliminating littleness and endearing the eternal spirit of man.

I would like to express my deep sense of gratitude to Shri J. K. Singh of M/s Abhijeet Publications who has readily agreed to publish this book with all care and seriousness of purpose in disseminating Rabindranath Tagore's songs on solidarity.

Sobdo Chakrabarti, my son, has sincerely dealt with the computer processing of the book. Love and best wishes, Sobdo.

I dedicate this book as a token of reverence to my elder brother, Shri Rongomoy Chakrabarti, whose devotion to studies always inspires me.

If the book contributes a little to the endless world of Rabindranath Tagore's songs on solidarity and appeals to everyone everywhere, I would murmur within myself his soul-stirring words: "Give me the strength lightly to bear my joys and sorrows."

Seemantika

MOHIT CHAKRABARTI

Seemanto Palli

Santiniketan—731 235

(W.B.) INDIA

Index to the Songs

Agnisikha, eso eso, ano ano alo.
Duhkhe sukhe ghare ghare grihadeep jwalo.
Ano sakti, ano deepti, ano santi, ano tripti,
Ano snigdha bhalobasa, ano nitya bhalo.
Eso punyapath beye eso he kalyani—
Subha supti, subha jagaran deho ani.
Duhkharate matribese jege thako nirnimeshe
Ananda-utsabe taba subhra hasi dhalo.

Come, come, Flame of fire, bring, bring light
In sorrow and happiness enkindle the lamp in every house.
Bring power, bring efflorescence, bring peace, bring contentment,
Bring serene love, bring the eternal good.
Come treading through the path of virtue, come O the Mother of Goodness—
Auspicious slumber, auspicious awakening do thou bring.
In the sorrowful night in the apparel of the mother, remain wide awake,
Shower thy pure laughter in the ceremony of joy.

Ekhano ghor bhange na tor ye, mele na tor ankhi—
Kantar bane phul phutechhe re Janis ne tui ta ki.
Ore alas, janis ne tui ta ki.
Jago ebar jago, bela katas na go.
Kathin pather seshe kothay agam bijan dese
O sei bandhu amar ekla achhe go, dis ne tare phanki.
Prakhar rabir tape na-hay sushka gagan kanpe,
Na-hay dagdha balu tapta anchale dik chari dik dhaki—
Pipasate dik chari dik dhaki.
Maner majhe chahi dekh re ananda ki nahi.
Pathe paye paye dukher bansari baje tore daki—
Madhur sure bajbe tore daki.

Even now your numbness does not slip away, eyes do not open up.
Flowers have bloomed in the forest of thorns—do you not know that?
O indolent, do you not know that?
Awake, awake now, O do not while away time.
At the end of the rugged path towards the lonely land inaccessible and unknown,
O that friend of mine remains alone, do not give him a slip.
May be with the heat of the blazing sun the dry sky trembles,
May be the burnt sand with its heated covering envelopes the four directions,

In thirst covers the four directions.

Looking into the mind, O behold if it is bereft of joy.

On the way the flute of sadness would play on calling you at every footstep—

In pleasant tunes would play on calling you.

Amar mukti aloy aloy ei akase
Amar mukti dhulay dhulay ghase ghase.
Dehamaner sudur pare hariye pheli apanare,
Ganer sure amar mukti urdhe bhase.
Amar mukti sarbajaner maner majhe,
Duhkhabipad-tuchchha-kara kathin kaje.
Biswadhatar yajnasala atmahomer bahni jwala—
Jeeban jena di ahuti mukti-ase.

In the festival of light is my freedom in this firmament,
My freedom is in the dust on the grass.
In the faraway embankments of the body and the mind do I lose myself,
In the tune of the song my freedom floats high.
My freedom is amidst the minds of all
In difficult activities that make sorrow and adversity insignificant
In the All Creator's school of sacrifice enkindle the fire of self-havan—
Let me sacrifice the life in the hope of emancipation.

Anek diner sunyata mor bharte habe
Mounabeenar tantra amar jagao sudharabe.
Basantasameere tomar phul-photano bani
Dik parane ani—
Dako tomar nikhil-utsabe.
Milansatadale
Tomar premer arup moorti dekhao bhubantale.
Sabar sathe milao amay, bhulao ahankar,
Khulao ruddhadwar
Purna karo pranatigourabe.

My void of many days would have to be filled in.
Awaken the strings of my silent *veena* with pleasing sound.
In the vernal wind let your flower-blooming message
Adorn my heart
Call on in your ceremony of the world.
In the union of the lotus
Show the exquisite image of your love in the world.
Make me in unison with all, forget pride,
Make the barred door open
Fill in with the glory of salutation.

Jago nirmal netre ratrir parapare,
Jago antarakshetre muktir adhikare.
Jago bhaktir tirthe pujapushper ghrane,
Jago unmukhachitte, jago amlanaprane,
Jago nandananritye sudhasindhur dhare,
Jago swarther prante premamandiradware.
Jago ujjwal punye, jago nischal ashe,
Jago nihsim sunye purner bahupashe.
Jago Brahmer name, jago kalyanakaje,
Jago durgamayatri duhkher abhisare,
Jago swarther prante premamandiradware.

Awake in eyes distinct on the other shore of night
Awake in the arena of the mind in the depth of freedom.
Awake in the pilgrimage of devotion in the fragrance of the flowers of worship.
Awake with the mind acquivered, awake with a heart serene
Awake in dance aesthetic beside the sea of juice,
Awake on the edge of the self at the door of the temple of love.
Awake with virtue resplendent, awake with hope unmoved
Awake in the endless void in the embrace of fullness
Awake in the abode of fearlessness, awake in the robe of struggle
Awake in the name of the Brahma, awake in auspicious deeds.
Awake O traveller unknown in the adventure of sorrow,
Awake on the edge of the self at the door of the temple of love.

Pantha, ekhano kena alasita anga—
Hero, pushpabane jage bihanga.
Gagan magan nandana-alok ullase,
Loke loke uthe pranataranga.
Ruddha hridayakakshe timire
Kena atmasukhaduhkhe sayan—
Jago jago, chalo mangalapathe—
Yatridale mili laho biswer sanga.

Traveller, why with idle limbs even now!
Behold, birds awake in the flower garden
The sky is rapt in the laughter of heavenly light
The waves of life surge in people everywhere.
In the closed room of the heart in darkness
Why are you laid in self-happiness and sorrow?
Awake, awake, tread on the auspicious path,
Take the companionship of the universe by being in
unison with the group of travellers.

Amar prane gabheer gopan maha-apan se ki,
Andhakare hathat tare dekhi.
Jabe durdam jhade agal khule pade,
Kar se nayan-'pare nayan jay go theki.
Jakhan ase param lagan takhan gagan-majhe
Tahari bheree baje.
Bidyut udbhase bedanari doot ase,
Amantraner banee jay hridaye lekhi.

O the great-endearing he is in my heart deep and undisclosed,
In darkness suddenly do I behold him,
When in uncontrolled storm the barrier drops,
O in whose eyes the sight is arrested!
When the great moment comes, then in the sky
It is his trumpet that plays on.
In the flash of lightning the messenger of pain himself
Comes and writes the message of welcome in the heart.

Nutan pran dao pranasakha, aji suprabhate.
Bishad sab karo dur nabin anande,
Prachin rajani naso nutan ushaloke.

Friend of my heart, give new life in today's auspicious morning.
In joy anew drive away all sorrow.
Put an end to the night old in the aura of the new dawn.

Otho otho re—bifale prabhat bahe jay je.
Melo ankhi, jago jago, theko na re achetan.
Sakalei tanr kaje dhaila jagatamajhe,
Jagila prabhatabayu, bhanu dhaila akasapathe.
Eke eke nam dhare dakichhen bujhi prabhu—
Eke eke phulguli tai phutiya uthichhe bane.
Suna se ahabanabani, chaho sei mukhapane—
Tanhar asis laye
Chalo re jai sabe tanr kaje.

Awake O awake—the morning passes in vain!
Open eyes, awake awake, O do not remain unconscious.
Everyone for His service rushed amidst the world,
The morning wind awoke, the sun rushed towards the path of the sky.
As if the Lord called on one by one by name—
So the flowers in the forest are a-bloom one by one.
Listen to that beckoning, look at that countenance.
Receiving His blessings, O let all of us depart for His service.

Akase	***dui hate prem bilay o ke.***
Se sudha	***gadiye gela loke loke.***
Gachhera	***bhare nila sabuj patay,***
Dharanee	***dhare nila apan mathay.***
Pakhira	***pakhay tare nila enke.***
Chhelera	***kudiye nila mayer buke,***
Mayera	***dekhe nila chheler mukhe.***
Se je oi	***duhkhasikhay uthla jwale,***
Se je oi	***asrudharay padla gale.***
Se je oi	***bideerna beer-hriday hate***
Bahila	***maranroopee jeebansrote.***
Se je oi	***bhangagadar tale tale***
Neche jay	***dese dese kale kale.***

O who is one who gives away love in both hands!
That juice melted down in every country
Trees filled in with that in green leaves
The earth held over its own head.
Flowers adorned all the body
Birds painted it in wings.
Boys picked it up on mothers' laps,
Mothers observed it in the boys' countenances.
O yonder it flashed out in the flame of sorrow,
O yonder it melted in the stream of tears.
O yonder from the piercing brave heart
It flowed in the deathlike stream of life.
O yonder with the rhythm of destruction and creation
It goes on dancing from time to time.

Andhar rajani pohala, jagat purila pulake.
Bimal prabhatakirane mililа dyulok bhulake.
Jagat nayan tuliya hridayaduyar khuliya
Herichhe hridayanathere apan hriday-aloke.
Premamukhahasi tanhari padichhe dharar anane—
Kusum bikasi uthichhe, sameer bahichhe kanane.
Sudheere andhar tutichhe, das dik phute uthichhe—
Jananir kole jena re jagichhe balika balake.
Jagat je dike chahichhe se dike dekhinu chahiya,
Heri se aseem madhuri hriday uthichhe gahiya.
Nabeen aloke bhatichhe, nabeen ashay matichhe,
Nabeen jeeban labhiya joy joy uthe triloke.

The dark night dawned, in joy was the world filled.
The pure morning sunlight made heaven in unison with the earth.
Raising the eyes and opening the door of the heart
The world is visualising the Lord of the heart in His own light of the heart.
His loving countenance in the mirror of the world is reflecting.
Flowers are blooming, the wind in the garden is blowing.
Darkness is very slowly being erased out, everywhere there is awakening,
In the lap of mother as it were girls and boys are waking.

Eyeing at the direction where the world is beholding,
I encountered endless beauty—the heart leaps up singing.
In new light everything is shining in intoxication of new hope.
Achieving new life, the slogan of victory pervades everywhere.

Tomar hater rakheekhani bandho amar dakhin hate
Surya jeman dharar kare alok-rakhi jaday prate.
Tomar asis amar kaje safal habe biswa-majhe,
Jwalbe tomar deepta sikha amar sakal bedanate.
Karma kari je hat laye karbandhan tare bandhe.
Faler asa sikal haye jadiye dhare jatil phande.
Tomar rakhee bandho anti—sakal bandhan jabe kati,
Karma takhan beenar mato bajbe madhur moorchhanate.

Fasten the *rakhee* of your hand in my right hand
In the same way as the morning sun entangles the *rakhee* of light on the earth's hand.
In my work your blessings will be successful amid the universe,
Enkindled will be your illumined flame in all my pains.
The hand with which I work is bound by the bindings of work.
The hope of success clasps up in the difficult trap like a chain.
Tightly fasten your rakhee—all the strings would be cut off,
Work then would play on like a *veena* in pleasant rhapsodies.

Bajre tomar baje bansi, se ki sahaj gan.
Sei surete jagba ami, dao more sei kan.
Bhulba na ar sahajete, sei prane man uthbe mete
Mrityu-majhe dhaka achhe je antaheen pran.
Se jhad jena sai anande chittabeenar tare
Saptasindhu das diganta nachao je jhankare.
Aram hate chhinna kare sei gabheere lao go more
Asantir antare jethay santi sumahan.

In thunder your flute plays on. Is that a simple song?
In that very tune would I awake, give me those ears.
No more would I forget in simplicity, the mind would be intoxicated with that life
Endlessly encapsulated in the midst of death.
May I, in joy, forbear that storm in the strings of the *veena* of my mind.
With resonance do you make the seven seas and the ten horizons dance.
Tearing off from comfort, O take me to that poignance
Where peace with all fine grandeur lies in the heart of disturbance.

Jagite habe re—
Mohanidra kabhu na rabe chiradin,
Tyajite haibe sukhasayan asanighoshane.
Jage tanr nyayadanda sarbabhubane,
Phire tanr kalachakra aseem gagane,
Jwale tanr rudranetra papatimire.

O we would have to awake!
The enchanted sleep will not last for ever
The happy bed would have to be given up in the electrifying call.
His scale of justice exists all over the world,
His wheel of Time moves in the endless sky,
His furious eyes burn in the darkness of sin.

Joy hok, joy hok naba arunoday.
Purbadiganchal hok jyotirmay.
Eso aparajita banee, asatya hani—
Apahrita sanka, apagata sangsay.
Eso nabajagrata pran, chirajoubanajayagan.
Eso mrityunjoy asa jadatwanasa—
Krandan dur hok, bandhan hok kshay.

Let victory, victory be to new sunrise.
Let the eastern horizon be full of lustre.
Come, the undefeated message by eliminating falsehood,
Striking fear, warding off doubt.
Come the newly awakened life, the victorious song of eternal youth,
Come the death-winning hope, the destroyer of passivity—
Let crying be eliminated, bondage unyoked.

Gaba tomar sure dao se beena jantra,
Sunba tomar banee dao se amar mantra.
Karba tomar seba dao se param sakti,
Chaiba tomar mukhe dao se achal bhakti.
Saiba tomar aghat dao se bipul dhairya,
Baiba tomar dhwaja dao se atal sthairya.
Neba sakal biswa dao se prabal pran,
Karba amay nihswa dao se premer dan.
Jaba tomar sathe dao se dakhin hasta,
Ladba tomar rane dao se tomar astra.
Jagba tomar satye dao sei ahaban.
Chhadba sukher dasya, dao dao kalyan.

Sing shall I with thy tune, give me that *veena*,
Listen shall I to thy message, give me that eternal vow.
I shall serve thee, give me that great strength,
I shall look at thee, give me that unmoved devotion.
Your strike shall I forbear, give me that profound patience,
Your flag shall I bear, give me that unmoved strength.
Win shall I all the world, give me that forceful life,
I shall make myself bereft of wealth, give me that gift of love.
I shall go with thee, give me that right hand,
I shall fight in thy battle, give me thy weapon.

Wake shall I with thy truth, give me that beckoning,
Leave shall I the bondage of happiness, give, give me goodness.

Purano janiya cheyo na amare adhek ankhir kone alas anyamane.

Apanare ami dite asi jei jeno jeno sei subha nimeshei

Jeerna kichhui nei kichhu nei, phele dei puratane.

Apanare dey jharna apan tyagarase uchchhali—

Lahare lahare nutan nutan arghyer anjali.

Madhabikunja bar bar kari banalakshmeer dala dey bhari—

Bar bar tar danamanjaree naba naba kshane kshane.

Tomar preme ye legechhe amay chira nutaner sur.

Sab kaje mor sab bhabanay jage chirasumadhur.

Mor dane nei deenatar les, yata nebe tumi nahi pabe sesh—

Amar diner sakal nimesh bhara asesher dhane.

Look at me not, knowing me old.

In the corners of your eyes half open, in the absent idle mind

When I come to submit myself

Know, know at that very auspicious moment

Nothing, nothing is tattered.

The old I leave off.

The fountain offers itself with the overflow of the stream of sacrifice,

In every wave are its new folded hands of offerings.

The grove of *madhabee* again and again

Fills in the tray of the goddess of forest,

Again and again her flowers of offering
At every moment turn newer and newer.
In your love I am thrilled
With the tune of the ever new,
In all my acts and in all my thoughts the ever pleasant awakes.
No poverty does my offering kiss,
The more will you take the less you will miss.
Every moment of my day is the bliss of the wealth of the endless.

Ke re oi dakichhe,
Sneher rab uthichhe jagate jagate—
Tora aay aay aay aay.
Tai anande bihanga gaan gahe
Prabhate se sudhaswar prachare.
Bishad tabe kena, asru bahe chokhe,
Shokakatar akul kena aji!
Kena niranandа, chalo sabe yai—
Purna habe asha.

Yonder who is calling?
The sound of affection is arisen everywhere in the world.
Come ye, come, come, come.
So the bird sings in joy.
The melodious voice does it disseminate in the morning.
Why sorrow, tears flow in your eyes,
Why afflicted pains of bereavement today,
Why bereft of joy? Let's go together.
Fulfilled will be expectations.

Tor apan jane chhadbe tore,
Ta bale bhabna kara chalbe na.
Tor ashalata padbe chhide,
Hayto re phal phalbe na.
Asbe pathe andhar neme, taibalei ki raibe theme—
O tui bare bare jwalbi bati,
Hayto bati jwalbe na.
Shune tomar mukher bani asbe ghire baner pranee—
Tabu hayto tomar apan ghare
Pashan hiya galbe na.
Bandha duar dekhli bale amni ki asbi chale—
Tor bare bare thelte habe,
Hayto duar talbe na.

Your own people will leave you,
For that, to ponder over would not do
Your creeper of hope will be torn apart
May be that nothing would be brought forth.
Darkness would descend on the way, would you remain motionless for that alone—
O you would time and again trim the lamp,
May be that the lamp would not bring forth light.
Hearing the message from your mouth, the forest animals will throng around,
Yet in your own room the strong heart would not possibly melt.
Seeing the closed door, would you come back in vain!
You would have to push again and again,
May be that the door would not move.

E Bharate rakho nitya Prabhu, taba shubha ahseerbad—
Tomar abhay, tomar ajit amrita bani,
Tomar sthir amar asha.
Anirban dharma alo sabar urdhe-jwalo jwalo,
Sankate durdine he,
Rakho tare aranye tomari pathe.
Bakshe bandhi dao tar barma taba nirbidar,
Nihshanke jena sanchare nirbhik.
Paper nirakhi joy nishtha tabu ray—
Thake taba charane atal biswase.

Lord, ever confer thy auspicious blessings upon this India—
Thy fearless, thy unvanquished nectar-like message,
Thy firm deathless expectations
Enkindle, O kindle light, the ever-illumined religion, above all,
In crisis and in rainy days,
Place it along the forest on thy path.
Encompass his breast with thy non-piercing armour
So that he might traverse sans fear.
Beholding the victory of vice, sincerity still persists—
With firm faith does adorn thy feet.

Prabhu, aji tomar dakshin hat rekho na dhaki.
Esechhi tomare he nath, parate rakhee.
Yadi bandhi tomar hate padba bandha sabar sathe,
Yekhane ye achhe kehai rabe na baki.
Aji yena bhed nahi ray apana pare,
Tomay yena ek dekhi he bahire ghare.
Toma-sathe ye bichchhede ghure bedai kende kende
Kshanek tare ghuchate tai tomare daki.

Lord, do not cover thy right hand today.
O Lord, I have come to adorn you with *rakhi.*
If I adorn it in your hand, I would be in unison with all
Nobody living anywhere would remain scared.
Let there be no difference between others and the self today,
O let me behold thee the same within me and outside.
The separation from thee with which I wander crying,
For a while I call on thee to shed off that.

Biswasathe yoge yethay bihara
Seikhane yog tomar sathe amaro.
Nayko bane, nay bijane, nayko amar apan mane—
Sabar yethay apan tumi he priya, sethay apan amaro.
Sabar pane yethay bahu pasara
Seikhanetei prem jagibe amaro.
Gopane prem ray na-ghare, alor mato chhadiye pade—
Sabar tumi anandadhan he priya, ananda sei amaro.

The unison with the world with which you wander,
There am I united with you.
Neither in the forest nor in solitude nor even in my own mind –
O dear where you are dear to all, you are also close to me there.
Where you stretch your hands towards all,
At that very place my love would also awake.
In secret, love does not reside inside, like light does it effulge away—
O dear you are a treasure of joy to all, that joy is mine as well.

More daki laye yao muktadware tomar biswer sabhate
Aji e mangalaprabhate.
Udayagiri hate uchche kaho more 'Timir lay hala deeptisagare—
Swartha hate jago, dainya hate jago, sab jadata hate jago jago re,
Satej unnata sobhate.'
Bahir karo taba pather majhe, baran karo more tomar kaje.
Nibid abaran karo bimochan, mukta karo sab tuchchha sochan,
Dhouta karo mama mugdha lochan tomar ujjwal subhrarochan
Nabeen nirmal bibhate.

Call on me and take me to the open door in the assembly of your world
Today on this auspicious morning.
From the rising mountain tell me aloud, 'Darkness is over in the sea of light—
Awake from your own self, from poverty do you awake, O awake, awake from all drabness
In the beauty of agile uprightness.'
If you expose me out amidst your path, engage me in your work.
Leave off the close covering, do away with all trifling repentance,
Wash my enamoured look with your bright and clear appreciation
In young and pure effulgence.

Purvagaganabhage
Dipta haila suprabhat
Tarunarunarage.
Subhra subha muhurta aji sarthak karo re,
Amrite bharo re—
Amitapunyabhagi ke
Jage ke jage.

In the eastern part of the sky
The auspicious morning effulged
In the aura of the young sun.
O make the white auspicious moment a success,
O fill it in the nectar
Who, the endless partner of virtue, awakes,
Who awakes?

Mon, jaga mangalaloke amal amritamoy naba aloke
Jyotibibhasita chokhe.
Hera gagan bhari jage sundar, jage tarange jeevanasagar—
Nirmal prate visver sathe jaga abhay asoke.

Awake, my mind, in the world of goodness in the new aura of purity and full of nectar
In eyes flooded with lustre.
Behold the Beautiful that adorns all through the sky, the sea of life awakes in waves—
Awake with the world in the clear morn, awake sans fear sans bereavement.

Apanare diye rachili re ki e apanari abaran,
Khule dekh dwar antare tar anandaniketan.
Mukti ajike nai kono dhare akas seo ye bandhe karagare,
Bishaniswase tai bhare ase niruddha samiran.
Thele de adal ghuchibe andhar—apanare phel dure—
Sahaje takhani jeeban tomar amrite uthibe pure.
Sunya kariya rakh tor bansi, bajabar yini bajaben asi—
Bhiksha na nibi takhani janibi bhara ache tor dhan.

What a covering of yours alone have you created by yourself!
Open the door and see in his heart the abode of joy.
Freedom is nowhere today, the sky even arrests in the prison house,
With poisoned breath the barred breeze is therefore filled up.
Push off the barrier, darkness would disappear—throw the self off—
Just at that moment your life would be brimmed in with nectar.
Keep your flute vacant, one to play on would arrive and play on—
Alms you won't beg, only then you would know your credited wealth.

Sabar majhare tomare sweekar kariba he.
Sabar majhare tomare hridaye bariba he.
Sudhu apanar mane nay, apan gharer kone nay,
Sudhu apanar rachanar majhe nahe—tomar mahima jetha ujjwal rahe
Sei saba-majhe tomare sweekar kariba he.
Dyuloke bhuloke tomare hridaye bariba he.

Sakali teyagi tomare sweekar kariba he.
Sakali grahan kariya tomare bariba he.
Kebali tomar stabe nay, sudhu sangeetarabe nay,
Sudhu nirjane dhyaner asane nahe –taba sangsar yekhane jagrata rahe,
Karme sethay tomare sweekar kariba he.
Priye apriye tomare hridaye bariba he.

Jani na baliya tomare sweekar kariba he.
Jani bale nath, tomare hridaye bariba he.
Sudhu jeebaner sukhe nay, sudhu prafullamukhe nay,
Sudhu sudiner sahaj suyoge nahe—dukhasok yetha andhar kariya rahe
Nata haye setha tomare sweekar kariba he.
Nayaner jale tomare hridaye bariba he.

O amidst all I would admit you.
O amidst all I would welcome you in the heart.
Neither in one's own room only. nor in the corners of one's room

Not in one's own creations, where your greatness remains effulgent,

O amidst that congregation I would accept you.

O in heaven and earth I would welcome you in the heart.

O sacrificing all, I would admit you.

O accepting all, I would welcome you in the heart.

Not only in your appreciation, in sounds of music only,

Not in the seat of lonely meditation but where your world remains awake

O there in work I would accept you

O I would welcome you, the endearing or not endearing, in the heart.

O for my ignorance I would admit you.

O as I know I would welcome you in the heart.

Not only in happiness of life, in smiling countenance only,

Not in easy chances of sunny days but where darkness wraps in sorrow and bereavement

O bowing down, I would accept you there.

O in tears I would welcome you in the heart.

Amra chash kari anande.
Mathe mathe bela kate sakal hate sandhe.
Roudra othe, brishti pade, banser bane pata nade,
Batas othe bhare bhare chasha matir gandhe.
Sabuj praner ganer lekha rekhay rekhay dey re dekha
Mate re kon tarun kabi nrityadodul chhande.
Dhaner sishe pulak chhote-- sakal dhara hese othe
Aghraneri sonar rode, purnimari chandre.

In joy we cultivate.
Days pass by from morn till evening.
The sun shines, rains fall, leaves move in the bamboo forest,
The air is filled in with the fragrance of cultivated soil.
O the writings of the young life is visible in countless lines
O who is that young poet intoxicated with the dancing swing of rhymes!
Joy runs through the paddy flowers, the whole earth is in merriment
In the sunshine of the very early winter or in the full-moon light.

Ar nahe ar nay.
Ami kari ne ar bhay.
Amar ghuchla kandan falla sadhan
Hala bandhan kshay.
Oi akase oi dake
Amay ar ke dhare rakhe,
Ami sakal duyar khulechhi aj
Yaba sakalamay.
Ora base base michhe
Sudhu mayajal ganthichhe,
Ora kee ye gone gharer kone
Amay dake pichhe.
Amar astra hala gada,
Amar barma hala para,
Ebar chhutbe ghoda paban bege
Karbe bhuban jay.

No more, no more.
No more do I fear.
My weeping is over, my meditation is fruitful,
My bondage is eliminated.
Yon the beckoning is there in the sky.
Who keeps me arrested any more?
All the doors have I opened today,
Towards all I go.
Sitting in vain,
They are preparing the garland of illusion.

O what do they count in the corner of the room
And beckon me behind!
Arms have I made,
Armours have I put on,
Now the horse will run like the speedy wind
And win the world.

Kebal thakis sare sare,
Pas ne kichhui hriday bhare.
Anandabhandarer theke doot ye tore gela deke—
Kone base dis ne sada, sab khoyali emni kare.
Jeebanke aj tol jagiye,
Majhe sabar ay agiye.
Chalis ne path mepe mepe apnake de nikhil byepe—
Yetuku din baki achhe katas ne ta ghumer ghore.

Aloof you only remain,
Receive nothing in fullness of heart.
O from the storehouse of joy the messenger called on you,
Sitting in the corner, no response did you give; everything did you lose thus.
Lift up life today,
Come forward amidst all.
Tread not the path controlled, deliver yourself all thro' the world—
Spend not in the swoon of slumber the rest of the day left out.

Jani nai go sadhan tomar bale kare.
Ami dhulay base khelechhi ei
Tomar dware.
Abodh ami chhilem bale yeman khusi elem chale,
Bhay kari ni tomay ami andhakare.
Tomar jnanee amay bale kathin tiraskare,
'Path diye tui asis ni ye, phire ya re.'
Pherar pantha bandha kare apni bandho bahur dore,
Ora amay mithya dake bare bare.

O knew I not what is called your meditation.
Sitting on the dust have I played
At your door
Fool as I was, I came back as I wished,
Afraid was I not of you in darkness.
In rude words the wise in you tells me,
'Along the path you came not, O go back.'
Closing the way to return, in the clasp of arms you bind me,
In vain do they call me again and again.

Habe joy, habe joy, habe joy re,
Ohe beer, he nirbhay.
Jayee pran, chirapran, jayee re anandagan,
Jayee prem, jayee kshem, jayee jyotirmay re.
E andhar habe kshay, habe kshay re,
Ohe beer, he nirbhay.
Chhado ghum, melo chokh, abasad dur hok,
Asar arunalok hok abhyuday re.

Victory, victory, O victory shall be.
O brave, O fearless.
Life is victorious, life is eternal, O victorious is the joyous muse,
Victory to love, victory to patience, O victory to the luminous one,
This darkness would diminish, O diminish it would,
O brave, O fearless.
Leave off slumber, open eyes, let all fatigue be fizzled out,
O let the aura of the sun of hope be effulged.

Ananderi sagar hate esechhe aj ban.
Dnar dhare aj bos re sabai, tan re sabai tan.
Bojha yata bojhai kari karba re par dukher taree,
Dheuer 'pare dharba padi—yay yadi yak pran.
Ke dake re pichhan hate, ke kare re mana,
Bhayer katha ke bale aj—bhay achhe sab jana.
Kon sape kon graher doshe sukher dangay thakba base.
Paler rasi dharba kashi, chalba geye gan.

From the very sea of joy tide has come today
O holding oars, be all seated today, pull on, O pull on.
With all burdens stacked, we would tide over the boat of sorrow,
On the waves shall we cross, be it at the cost of life!
O who calls from behind, O who forbids,
Who speaks about fear today—all fear is known.
For which curse and fault of the planets would we remain seated in the lap of happiness!
Tightly would we hold the rope of the sail and go on singing.

Rakho rakho re jeebane jeebanaballabhe,
Pranamane dhari rakho nibid anandabandhane.
Alo jwalo hridayadeepe atinibhrita antaramajhe,
Akulia dao pran gandhachandane.

Keep, O keep the friend of life in the life.
Hold him heart and soul in close strings of joy.
Enkindle the lamp of the heart amid the very secret mind.
With fragrant sandal-paste, flood away life.

Nibid ghana andhare jwalichhe dhrubatara.
Man re mor, pathare hos ne disehara.
Bishade haye mriyaman bandha na kariyo gan,
Safal kari tolo pran tutiya mohakara.
Rakhiyo bal jeebane, rakhiyo chira-asa,
Sobhan ei bhubane rakhiyo bhalobasa.
Sangsarer sukhe dukhe chaliya yeyo hasimukhe,
Bhariya sada rekho buke tanhari sudhadhara.

Amidst deep dense darkness the polestar is burning.
O my friend, do not lose direction in the sea.
Being distressed in grief, stop not your music,
Turn life into a success by breaking off the prison of enchantment.
Have strength in life, keep hope for eternity.
Enrich this beautiful world with love.
In the weal and woe of the world, bid farewell with a happy countenance.
Always feel in the breast with this stream of juice.

Anandadhara bahichhe bhubane,
Dinarajanee kata amritaras uthali yay ananta gagane.
Pan kare rabi sasee anjali bhariya—
Sada deepta rahe akshay jyoti—
Nitya purna dhara jeebane kirane.
Basiya achha kena apan-mane,
Swarthanimagan kee karane?
Chari dike dekho chahi hriday prasari,
Kshudra duhkha sab tuchchha mani
Prem bhariya laho sunya jeebane.

The stream of joy is flowing in the world.
In what profusion the nectar-juice overflows the unending sky!
With folded palms the sun and the moon drink-
The everlasting aura remains ever enlightened.
With light in life the earth is eternally filled in.
Why seated alone in your own mind,
Why immersed in your own interest?
Look around with an expanded heart,
Considering every petty sorrow insignificant,
Fill in the empty life with love.

Akas hate khasla tara andhar rate pathahara.
Prabhat tare khunjte yabe—dharar dhulay khunje pabe
Trine trine sisiradhara.
Dukher pathe gela chale—nibla alo, maran jwale.
Rabir alo neme ese miliye nebe bhalobese,
Duhkha takhan habe sara.

Stars dropped from the sky in the way-lost dark night.
Morning would go to find out, in the dust of the earth would be found
The flow of dews is over the grassland.
It departed towards the path of sorrow--the light was put off, death burns
Coming down, the light of the sun would be in loving unison,
Then sorrow would come to an end.

Agune hala agunmay.
Joy aguner joy.
Mithya yata hriday jude eibela sab yak-na pude,
Maran-majhe tor jeebaner hok re parichay.

Agun ebar challa re sandhane
Kalanka tor konkhane ye lukiye achhe prane.
Adal tomar yak re ghuche, lajja tomar yak re muchhe,
Chiradiner mato tomar chhai haye yak bhay.

In fire everything was full of fire.
Victory, victory to fire!
Let all falsehood of the heart be burnt right now,
O let the identity of your life be amidst death!

O fire now is in quest,
O where are your blemishes hidden in the heart today!
Let all your coverings be eliminated, let your shyness be erased out,
Let your fear be turned into ashes for ever.

Bhay karba na re bidaybedanare.
Apan sudha diye bhare deba tare.
Chokher jale se ye nabeen rabe, dhyaner manimalay se ye gantha habe,
Parba buker hare.
Nayan hate tumi asbe prane, milbe tomar banee amar gane.
Birahabyathay bidhur dine dukher aloy tomay nebo chine
E mor sadhana re.

O fear shall I not the pains of farewell.
With my own elixir I would fill it in.
O it would remain new with tears, with the gems of meditation it would be sewn
I would put it on in the garland of the breast.
From the eyes you would come to the heart, your message will merge in my muse.
In sordid days of the pains of dissociation, I would identify you in the light of sorrow—
O this is my worship!

Nayan chhede gele chale, ele sakal-maje—
Tomay ami harai yadi tabu harao na ye.
Furay yabe milanarati tabu nitya sather sathi
Lage tomar paoyar haoya, eso swapanasaje.
Tomar sudharaser dhara marmapathe ese
Byathare mor uchhal kari nayane yay bhese.
Srabane mor naba naba suniyechhile ye sur taba
Beena theke biday niye, chitte amar baje.

Bidding farewell to my eyes, you have departed and came amidst all.
If I lose you, you are never lost.
The night of union wanes, yet the constant companion
The air of having you do I feel, come in the apparel of dreams.
The flow of your pleasantries comes to the core of sentiment,
Making my pain exuberant, plies in the eyes a-floating.
The new tunes that you made me listen,
Bidding adieu to the *veena,* ring in my mind.

Prane khusir tufan uthechhe.
Bhay-bhabanar badha tutechhe.
Duhkhake aj kathin bale jadiye dharte buker tale
Udhao haye hriday chhutechhe.
Hethay karo thnai habe na mane chhila ei bhabana,
Duar bhenge sabai jutechhe.
Yatan kare apanake ye rekhechhilem dhuye meje,
Anande se dhulay lutechhe.

The hurricane of joy has surged in life,
Gone are the constraints of fear and thought.
To clasp sorrow under the breast as a stern one
The heart has run away in disappearance.
No shelter here would be for anyone.
So was the thought in the mind.
Breaking open the door, everyone has assembled.
So caressingly as I kept myself wasted and brushed.
Now he is on the dust in joy.

Aji heri sangsar amritamay.
Madhur paban, bimal kiran, fulla ban,
Madur bihagakaladhwani.
Kotha hate bahila sahasa pranabhara premahillol, aha—
Hridayakusum uthila futi pulakabhare.
Ati ascharya dekho sabe—deenaheen kshudra hridayamajhe
Aseem jagatswami biraje sundar sobhan!
Dhanya ei manabajeeban, dhanya biswajagat,
Dhanya tar prem, tini dhanya, dhanya.

The present world do I behold today full of nectar.
The air pleasant, the light pure, the merry forest,
The pleasing sound of the call of birds,
Ah, the swing of heart-filling love suddenly blew wherefrom none knows!
The flower of the heart bloomed in joy.
Behold, ye all, what a surprise—amid the little heart poor and despised
The endless Lord of the world is adorned lovely and serene!
Thankful is the human life, thankful the universe,
Glorious is His love, endlessly glorious He is.

He chiranutan, aji e diner pratham gane
Jeeban amar uthuk bikasi tomar pane.
Tomar baneete seemaheen asa, chiradibaser pranamayee bhasha—
Kshayaheen dhan bhari dey man tomari dane.
E subhalagane jaguk gagane amritabayu,
Anuk jeebane nabajanamer amal ayu.
Jeerna ya-kichhu yaha-kichhu ksheen nabeener majhe hok ta bileen—
Dhuye yak yata purano malin
Naba aloker snane.

O the ever new, in this first song today,
Let my life be effulged towards you.
Unending hope, living language of eternal days is in your message
With your gift wealth sans decay fulfils the mind.
In this auspicious moment let nectar-like wind arise in the sky.
Let it bring in life serene longevity of new life.
Whatever is tattered, whatever is in decay, let it be eliminated amongst the young—
Let everything old and dirty
Be washed away in the bathing of new light.

Premanande rakho purna amare dibasarat.
Biswabhubane nirakhi satata sundar tomare,
Chandra-surya-kirane tomar karun nayanapat.
Sukhasampade kari he pan taba prasadabari,
Dukhasankate paras pai taba mangalahat.
Jeebane jwalo amar deep taba ananta asa,
Maran-ante hauk tomari charane suprabhat.
Laho laho mama sab ananda, sakal preeti-geeti—
Hridaye bahire ekmatra amar nath.

With joy of love thou dost keep me filled in day and night.
All the time do I behold thee beautiful in the universe.
The eye-lids are piteous with the light of the moon and the sun.
Thy water of gifts do I drink in happiness and affluence.
In sorrow and danger do I feel the touch of thy auspicious hands.
Enkindle thy eternal lamp in the life with boundless hope.
Let good morning usher forth at the end of death at thy feet.
Take, take all my joys, all love and songs.
Beyond my heart, thou art my lone Lord.

Ore bheeru, tomar hate nai bhubaner bhar.
Haler kachhe majhi achhe, karbe taree par.
Tufan yadi ese thake tomar kiser day—
Cheye dekho dheuer khela, kaj ki bhabanay.
Asuk-nako gahan rati, hok-na andhakar—
Haler kachhe majhi achhe, karbe taree par.
Paschime tui takiye dekhis meghe akas doba,
Anade tui puber dike dekh-na tarar sobha.
Sathi yara achhe tara tomar apan ba'le
Bhaba ki tai raksha pabe tomari oi kole.
Uthbe re jhad, dulbe re buk, jagbe hahakar—
Haler kachhe majhi achhe karbe taree par.

O coward, the burden of the world rests not on you.
The oarsman is nearby the oars, and he'll sail the boat across.
If the storm comes, what worry do you have?
Behold the play of waves. What's the use of thoughts?
Let the dense night come, let darkness be dominant—
The oarsman is nearby the oars, and he'll sail the boat across.
Behold the western sky immersed in the cloud,
Just behold in joy the beauty of stars in the east.
As the comrades you have are your own,
Do you think that they are assured of safety in your lap?
The storm will start, the heart will swing, agonies will wail—
The oarsman is nearby the oars, and he'll sail the boat across.

Akase tor temni achhe chhuti,
Alas yena na ray dana duti.
Ore pakhi, ghana baner tale
Basa tore bhuliye rakhe chhale,
Ratri tore mithye kare bale—
Sithil kabhu habe na tor muthi.
Janis ne ki kiser asa cheye
Ghumer ghore uthis geye geye.
Janis ne ki bhorer andhar-majhe
Alor asa gabheer sure baje,
Alor asa gopan rahe na ye—
Ruddha kundir bandhan fele tuti.

Your freedom is there in the sky as it is
Let not the two wings remain idle
O bird, in the dense forest
The nest makes you forgetful in elusiveness
The night falsely tells you--
Your fist will never be loose.
Know ye not with what hope
You go on singing in the drowsiness of slumber.
Know ye not amidst the darkness at dawn
The hope of light rings in poignant tunes,
The hope of light does not remain a secret--
It tears off the string of the closed bud.

Kshata yata kshati yata michhe hate michhe,
Nimesher kusankur pade rabe neeche.
Kee hala na, kee pele na, ke taba sodhe ni dena
Se sakali mareechika milaibe pichhe.
Ei-ye herile chokhe aparoop chhabi
Arun gaganatale prabhater rabi—
Ei to param dan safal karila pran,
Satyer anandaroop
Ei to jagichhe.

As there are wounds and losses from falsehood to falsehood,
The grass-bud of the moment will lag behind.
What was not made, what not received, who repaid not the debt,
Mirage as all these are will afterwards disappear.
This exquisite picture that you just behold—
The morning sun in the red sky—
This is the great gift that made life successful.
The image of the joy of truth is
Just now waking!

Dukher katha tomay baliba na, dukh bhulechhi o karaparase.

Ya-kichhu diyechha tai peye he Nath, sukhe achhi, achhi harashe.

Ananda-asar e madhur bhaba, hetha ami achhi e kee sneha taba—

Tomar chandrama tomar tapan madhur kiran barashe.

Kata naba hasi fute fulabane pratidin nabaprabhate.

Prati nisi kata graha kata tara tomar neerab sabhate.

Jananeer sneha suhrider preeti sata dhare sudha dhale niti niti,

Jagater premamadhuramadhuri dubay amritarase.

Kshudra mora tabu na jani maran, diyechha tomar abhay saran—

Sok tap sab hay he haran tomar charanadarase.

Pratidin yena bade bhalobasa, pratidin mite praner pipasa—

Pai naba pran—jage naba asa naba naba naba-barashe.

The words of sorrow I would not tell, with the touch of that hand I have forgotten sorrow.

Lord, happy and glad am I on receipt of whatever you have given.

A joyous residence is this pleasant earth, what an affection of yours that I am here!

Your moon and the sun shower pleasing light.

What a lot of new smile effulges in this garden of flowers everyday in the new morning,

What a profusion of planets and stars every night adorn your silent assembly!
The mother's affection and the friend's love regularly pour juice in a hundred streams,
The elegance of sweet love of the world drowns in the lake of nectar.
Tyroes though we are, yet we know no death, your fearless refuge you have offered
Bereavement and achings—all are lost at the sight of your feet
As if love grows everyday, everyday the thirst of the heart is quenched—
A new life do I get, new hope awakes in newer new years.

Ye dhrubapada diyechha bandhi biswatane
Milabo tai jeebanagane.
Gagane taba bimal neel—hridaye laba tahari mil,
Santimayee gabheer banee neerab prane.
Bajay usha niseethakule ye geetabhasha
Se dhwani niye jagibe mor nabeen asa.
Fuler mato sahaj sure prabhat mama uthibe pure,
Sandhya mama se sure yena marite jane.

The permanent tune that you have strung in the global tune
In the song of life would I unite it.
In the clear blue sky of yours I would unite it in my heart
In silent life the peaceful poignant message.
The language of music that the dawn plays on in the shore of night,
With that sound will my young hope arise.
With easy tunes like flowers, my morning would be filled in.
Let my evening know how to die in that tune.

Bhuban haite bhubanabasi eso apan hridaye.
Hridayamajhe hridayanath achhe nitya sath sath—
Kotha firichha dibarat, hero tanhare abhaye.
Hetha chira anandadham, hetha bajichhe abhay nam,
Hetha puribe sakal kam nibhrita amrita-alaye.

Come to your own heart, O resident of the world!
The Lord of the heart is amid the heart all the time.
Where are you roaming day and night? Behold Him fearlessly.
The eternal abode of joy is here, the fearless name is ringing at this place.
All desires would be fulfilled here in the nectar-abode of silence.

Parbi naki yog dite ei chhande re
Khase yabar, bhese yabar, bhangbari anande re.
Patiya kan sunis na ye dike dike gagan-majhe
Maranbeenay kee sur baje tapan-tara-chandre re—
Jwaliye agun dheye dheye jwalbari anande re.
Pagal-kara ganer tane dhay ye kotha kei ba jane,
Chay na fire pichhan-pane, ray na bandha bandhe re—
Lute yabar, chute yabar, chalbari anande re.
Sei ananda-charan-pate chhay ritu ye nritye mate,
Plaban bahe yay dharate baran geete gandhe re—
Fele debar, chhede debar, marbari anande re.

O would you be able to join in this rhythm

In the joy of being dropped, floated away, and, of course, being broken?

With ears alert you listen not that amid the sky at every direction

What tune in the deadly *veena* plays on in the sky and the stars and the moon!

By enkindling the fire in the joy of being burnt in a rush,

None knows where he rushes on in the tune of the intoxicating song.

Behind he looks not, nor does he remain in cares and constraints.

With the joy of being enraptured, rushed on or moved

In that joyous setting of feet, the six seasons are

absorbed in dancing.
The flood sweeps on the world with the efflorescence of the song of invocation
In the joy of dropping, drooping or dying!

Dhyan nimagna neerab nagna
Nischal taba chitta;
Nihswa gagane biswa bhubane
Nihsesh sab bitta.
Rasaheen taru, nirjeeb maru,
Pabane garje rudra damaru,
Oi chari dhar kare hahakar
Dharabhandar rikta.
Taba tapa-tape hero sabe kanpe,
Debalok hala klanta.
Indrer megh, nahi tar beg,
Barun karun santa.
Durdine ane nirday bayu,
Sanghar kare kananer ayu,
Bhay hay dekhi, nikhil habe ki
Jadadanaber bhritya.
Jago fule fale naba trinadale
Tapas, lochan melo he.
Jago manaber asay bhashay,
Nacher charan felo he.
Jago dhane dhane, jago gane gane,
Jago sangrame, jago sandhane,
Aswashara udas parane
Jagao udar nritya.
Bhulechhe chhanda, bhaloy manda
Ekakar tai hay re.
Kadarya tai karichhe badai,

Dharanee lajja pay re.
Pinake tomar dao tankar,
Bheeshane madhure dik jhankar,
Dhulay misak ya kichhu dhular,
Jayee hok yaha nitya.

Rapt in meditation, silent, bare,
Motionless is your mind,
In the poor sky in the universe
Exhausted is all wealth.
Trees sans juice, the passive desert,
The violent drum roars in the wind.
Yon wailings all around,
Empty is the store of the earth.
With the heat of your meditation, behold, everyone trembles,
Tired became the world of gods.
The cloud of rain-god is without velocity,
Rains piteous and exhausted.
The kindless wind brings forth evil days,
Kills the longevity of the flower garden,
Seeing this, fear creeps in:
Will the world become the servant of the demon of matter?
Awake in flowers and fruits, in new grass,
O saint, open your eyes.
Awake in the hope and language of mankind,

O step on with dancing feet!
Awake in wealth and crop, in songs awake,
Awake in struggle, in quest awake,
In eccentric life sans assurance
Arouse unrestricted dance.
No accord in rhythm in between good and bad,
Alas, everything is in fusion!
That is why ugliness displays pride.
O the world is ashamed!
Beat your drum,
Let there be the sound of the violent and the pleasant,
Let everything of dust be in unison with dust,
Let what is eternal be victorious.

Aloy alokmay kare he ele alor alo.
Amar nayan hate andhar milala milala.
Sakal akas sakal dhara anande hasite bhara,
Ye-dik pane nayan meli bhalo sabi bhalo.
Tomar alo gachher patay nachiye tole pran.
Tomar alo pakhir basay jagiye tole gan.
Tomar alo bhalobese padechhe mor gaye ese,
Hridaye mor nirmal hat bulala bulala.

Thou hast come, O Light of light, flooding with light
Darkness from my eyes disappeared.
All the sky and the world are full of joy and laughter.
Where'er do I feast my eyes, everything is all right.
Thy light makes leaves of trees dancing in life.
Thy light arouses songs in the nests of birds.
Thy light has lovingly fallen on my body.
Thy clear hands soothed my heart.

Ei abaran kshay habe go kshay habe,
E dehaman bhumanandamay habe.
Chokhe amar mayar chhaya tutbe go,
Biswakamal prane amar futbe go,
E jeebane tomari Nath, jay habe.
Rakta amar biswatale nachbe ye,
Hriday amar bipul prane banchbe ye.
Kanpbe tomar alo-beenar tare se,
Dulbe tomar taramanir hare se,
Basana tar chhadiye giye lay habe.

This veil would be emaciated, O emaciated it would be!
Full of the joy of the earth this body and mind would be.
O the shadow of maya in my eyes would vanish,
The lotus of the world in my heart would bloom.
Lord, in this life thou alone wouldst attain victory.
My blood would dance in the rhythm of the world,
My heart would live in endless lives.
It would tremble in thy string of the veena of light,
It would swing in thy necklace of the gems of stars,
Its aspirations would end in scatterings.

Tomar kachhe e bar magi maran hate yena jagi
Ganer sure.
Yemni nayan meli yena matar stanyasudha-hena
Nabeen jeeban dey go pure ganer sure.
Sethay taru trina yata
Matir bansi hate othe ganer mato.
Alok setha dey go ani
Akaser anandabanee,
Hridaymajhe beday ghure ganer sure.

This boon do I pray to thee, let me rise from death
In the tune of songs.
When I open my eyes, like the breastmilk of the mother
The new life is filled with the tunes of songs.
All the trees and grass there
Awake like songs from the flute of the soil
The light there brings along
The message of the joy of the sky
And roams in the heart in the tunes of songs.

Bhay hate taba abhayamajhe nutan janam dao he.
Deenata hate akshay dhane, sangsay hate satyasadane,
Jadata hate nabeen jeebane nutan janam dao he.
Amar ichchha haite Prabhu, tomar ichchhamajhe—
Amar swartha haite Prabhu, taba mangalamajhe—
Anek haite eker dore, sukhadukh hate santikrode—
Ama hate Nath, tomate more nutan janam dao he.

From fear to thy fearlessness, O deliver me to the new birth!
From poverty to abundant wealth, from doubt to the abode of truth,
From drabness to young life, O deliver me to the new birth!
Lord, from my wilfulness to the desire amidst thee,
Lord, from my interest to thy good deeds,
From a lot to the string of one, from happiness and sorrow to the lap of peace,
Lord, from me to thee, O deliver me to the new birth!

Jagrata biswakolahal-majhe
Tumi gambheer, stabdha, santa, nirbikar,
Paripurna mahajnan.
Toma-pane dhay pran sab kolahal chhadi,
Chanchal nadee yeman dhay sagare.

Amidst the awakening noise of the universe
Thou art serene, silent, calm, sans reaction,
Total erudition.
Life rushes towards thee, leaving all noise
As a restless river rushes towards the sea.

Dhane jane achhi jadaye hay,
Tabu jano man to.nare chay.
Antare achha he antarayamee,
Ama cheye amay janichha swami—
Sab sukhe dukhe bhule thakay
Jano mama man tomare chay.
Chhadite pari ni ahankare,
Ghure mari sire bahiya tare,
Chhadite parile banchi ye hay—
Tumi jano man tomare chay.
Ya achhe amar sakali kabe
Nija hate tumi tuliya labe—
Sab chhede sab paba tomay.
Mane mane man tomare chay.

In wealth and people, alas, I am entangled,
Yet thou knowest that my mind wants thee.
In the heart, O traveller of the heart, thou art.
Lord, thou knowest me better than I.
In forgetting all happiness and sadness
Know ye that my mind wants thee.
Pride could I not forsake,
Bearing it on the head do I wander.
O I could survive if I could forsake it.
Thou knowest that my mind wants thee.
Whatever do I have would all be taken away
By thee at a time I know not.
By forsaking all would I have thee,
Aside does the mind want thee.

Kee bhay abhayadhame, tumi maharaja—bhay yay taba name.
Nirbhaye ayut sahastra lok dhay he,
Gagane gagane sei abhayanam gay he.
Taba bale kara balee yare kripamay,
Lokabhay bipad mrityubhay dur hay tar.
Asa bikase, sab bandhan ghuche, nitya amritaras pay he.

What fear is there, thou art the Great King, in thy name fear disappears.
O millions of people fearlessly rush,
O they sing that fearless name in the entire sky.
He whom you, the piteous one, strengthen with thy strength,
Becomes free from people, danger and death.
Hope effulges, all barriers are no more, O he is ever blessed with the juice of the nectar.

Mora satyer 'pare man aji kariba samarpan.
Joy joy satyer joy.
Mora bujhiba satya, pujiba satya, khunjiba satyadhan.
Joy joy satyer joy.
Yadi duhkha dahite hay tabu mithyachinta nay.
Yadi dainya bahite hay tabu mithyakarma nay.
Yadi danda sahite hay tabu mithyabakya nay.
Joy joy satyer joy.

Mora mangalakaje pran aji kariba sakale dan.
Joy joy mangalamoy.
Mora labhiba punya, sobhiba punye, gahiba punyagan.
Joy joy mangalamoy.
Yadi duhkha dahite hay tabu asubhachinta nay.
Yadi dainya bahite hay tabu asubhakarma nay.
Yadi danda sahite hay tabu asubhabakya nay.
Joy joy mangalamoy.

Sei abhaya Brahmanam aji mora sabe lailum—
Yini sakal bhayer bhay.
Mora kariba na sok ya habar hok, chaliba Brahmadham.
Joy joy Brahmer joy.
Yadi duhkha dahite hay tabu nahi bhay, nahi bhay.
Yadi dainya bahite hay tabu nahi bhay, nahi bhay.
Yadi mrityu nikat hay tabu nahi bhay, nahi bhay.
Joy joy Brahmer joy.

Mora ananda-majhe man aji kariba bisarjan.
Joy joy anandamoy.
Sakal drisye sakal biswe anandaniketan.
Joy joy anandamoy.
Ananda chitta-majhe ananda sarbakaje,
Ananda sarbakale duhkhe bipadajale,
Ananda sarbaloke mrityubirahe soke—
Joy joy anandamoy.

To truth we would submit our mind today.
Victory, victory, victory to truth!
We would understand truth, worship truth, seek true wealth.
Victory, victory, victory to truth!
If inflicted in sorrow, even then let there be no false thought.
If poverty is to be carried on, even then let there be no false accomplishment.
If punishment is to be tolerated, even then let there be no telling a lie.
Victory, victory, victory to truth!
In auspicious activity we would sacrifice our lives today.
We would achieve virtue, adorn in virtue, sing virtuous songs.
Victory, victory, victory to the All Good!
If inflicted in sorrow, even then let there be no ominous thought.
If poverty is to be carried on, even then let there be no

ominous activity.

If punishment is to be tolerated, even then let there be no ominous utterance.

Victory, victory, victory to the All Good!

That fearless name of the Brahma did all of us endear today

He is the fear of all fear.

We would not be bereaved, let anything to befall might happen, to the abode of the Brahma we would proceed.

Victory, victory, victory to the Brahma.

If inflicted in sorrow, even then no fear, no fear.

If poverty is to be carried on, even then no fear, no fear.

If death comes near, even then no fear, no fear.

Victory, victory, victory to the Brahma!

Amidst joy we would sacrifice our mind.

Victory, victory, victory to the All Joy!

In all scenery, in all thro' the universe is the abode of joy.

Victory, victory, victory to the All Joy!

Joy abides in the mind, joy in every action,

Joy everywhere, in dissociation and bereavement from death—

Victory, victory, victory to the All Joy!

Pantha ekhano kena alasita anga—
Hero, pushpabane jage bihanga.
Gagan magan nandan-alok ullase,
Loke loke uthe pranataranga.
Ruddha hridayakakshe timire
Kena atmasukhaduhkhe sayan—
Jago jago, chalo mangalapathe
Yatridale mili laho biswer sanga.

Traveller, why with idle limbs even now?
Behold, birds awake in the flower garden.
The sky is rapt in the laughter of heavenly light,
The waves of light surge in people everywhere.
In the closed room of the heart in darkness
Why are you laid in self-happiness and sorrow?
Awake, awake, tread on the auspicious path,
Take the companionship of the universe by being in unison with the group of travellers.

Jananeer dware aji oi suna go sankha baje.
Theko na theko na, ore bhai, magan mithya kaje.
Arghya bhariya ani dharo go pujar thali,
Ratanapradeepakhani yatane ano go jwali,
Bhari laye dui pani bahi ano phuladali,
Mar ahabanabanee ratao bhubanamajhe.
Aji prasanna pabane nabeen jeeban chhutichhe.
Aji prafulla kusume naba sugandha uthichhe.
Aji ujjwal bhale tolo unnata matha,
Nabasangeetatale gao gambheer gatha,
Paro malya kapale nabapallab-gantha,
Subha sundar kale sajo sajo naba saje.

On the door of the mother O listen the concshell plays on there.
Remain not, do not remain O brother entangled in sham work.
O hold on with filled in palms the tray of flowers for worship
O carefully bring the jewelled lamp trimmed on,
With two palms filled up, carry forth the casket of flowers,
Disseminate the message of welcome of the mother amidst the world.
Today the new life is running in the delightful wind.
Today new fragrance is emanating from joyous flowers.
Today raise the erect head with bright forehead.

With the tunes of new songs, sing sombre ballads
Decorate the forehead with the garland stitched in new leaves,
Dress, dress yourself in new dresses in the auspicious and lovely time.

Sei to ami chai—

Sadhana ya sesh have mor se bhabana to nai.

Faler tare nay to khonja, ke baibe se bisham bojha—Yei fale fal dhulay fele abar phul phutai.

Emni kare mor jeebane aseem byakulata,

Nitya nutan sadhanate nitya nutan byatha.

Pelei se to furiye feli, abar ami du hat meli—

Nitya deoya furay na ye, nitya neoya tai.

That's what I want

The thought that my worship would end is no more.

It's not a search for the result. Who would bear that hard burden!

Throwing off the outcome in the dust I bring forth flowers again.

In this way unending restlessness adorns my life,

Newer worship everyday welcomes newer pains daily.

O whenever I receive I spend it, again do I unfold my two hands—

O to offer everyday never ends, that's the reason for receiving daily.

Asantaler matir 'pare lutiye raba,
Tomar charan-dhulay dhulay dhusar haba.
Kena amay man diye ar dure rakha?
Chirajanam eman kare bhuliyo nako.
Asammane ano tene paye taba.
Tomar charan-dhulay dhulay dhusar haba.
Ami tomar yatridaler raba pichhe,
Sthan diyo he amay tumi sabar niche.
Prasad lagi kata loke ase dheye,
Ami kichhui chaiba na to, raiba cheye—
Sabar seshe baki ya ray tahai laba.
Tomar charan-dhulay dhulay dhusar haba.

Beneath thy seat prostrated shall I lie on the ground.
With the dust of thy feet, dusty shall I be.
Why do thou keepest me away with honour?
Make me not so enamoured for ever.
Pull me adrift towards thy feet in disgrace.
Behind the group of thy travellers shall I remain,
O place me to the lowest of all.
For thy offerings, so many people rush towards thee.
Nothing do I pray but stare at thee merely—
And accept the left-outs whatsoever by all.
With the dust of thy feet dusty shall I be.

Amar ya achhe ami sakal dite pari ni tomare nath—
Amar laj bhay, amar man apaman, sukh dukh bhabana.
Majhe rayechhe abaran kata sata, katamata—
Tai kende firi, tai tomare na pai,
Mane theke yay tai he maner bedana.
Yaha rekhechhe tahe kee sukh—
Tahe kende mari, tahe bhebe mari.
Tai niye yadi tomare pai kena ta dite pari na.
Amar jagater sab tomare deba, diye tomare neba—basana.

I could not offer thee all I have, O Lord!
My shame and awe, grace and disgrace,
My thoughts on happiness and sorrow
A thousand coverings are there
Amidst these in many a form.
So I roam a-weeping and so I fail to be with thee.
The pangs of my heart thus remain in my heart.
What happiness is there with what I have?
And with that I go on crying and thinking.
Why do I fail to offer thee when I encounter thee with these?
The world of all of mine shall I offer thee and win thee, my aspirations.

Aguner parasmani chhonao prane.
E jeeban punya karo dahan-dane.
Amar ei dehakhani tule dharo,
Tomar oi debalayer pradeep karo—
Nisidin alok-sikha jwaluk gane.
Andharer gaye gaye paras taba
Sara rat fotak tara naba naba.
Nayaner dristi hate ghuchbe kalo,
Yekhane padbe sethay dekhbe alo—
Byatha mor uthbe jwale urdha-pane.

Give a touch in life with the touchstone of fire,
Make this life holy with the gift of burning.
Hold up this body of mine,
Make me a lamp in that abode of gods in thee.
Let the flame of light burn in songs day and night.
Let thy touch in every sphere of darkness
Bloom new stars all night.
Darkness will diminish from eyesight.
Whatever it feasts, it will see light.
Upwards will my pain effulge.

Duyare dao more rakhiya nitya kalyan-kaje he.
Firiba ahaban maniya tomari rajyer majhe he.
Majiya anukhan lalase raba na padiya alase,
Hayechhe jarjar jeeban byartha dibaser laje he.
Amare rahe yena na ghiri satata bahutar sangsaye,
Bibidh pathe yena na firi bahul-sangraha-asaye.
Anek nripatir sasane na rahi sankita asane,
Firiba nirbhayagourabe tomari bhrityer saje he.

O keep me close to the door in good deeds everyday!
O I will carry out thy orders and wander amidst thy kingdom!
By ever involving in temptation, I would not remain in idleness.
O life has been shattered in the shame of baffled days!
In senseless doubts of diverse kinds let me not be encircled.
In manifold hopes of savings, let me not tread separate avenues.
O in fearless glory I will wander in the guise of thy servant alone!

Duhkha diye metaba duhkha tomar,
Snan karaba atal jale bipul bedanar.
Mor sangsar diba ye jwali, sodhan habe ye moher kali,
Maranbyatha diba tomar charane upahar.

With sorrow would I appease thy sorrow,
I would wash in the depthless water of immense pain.
I would burn my world, the darkness of enchantment would be purified,
I would present the pain of death at thy feet.

Jani tomar preme sakal premer banee mese,
Ami seikhanetei mukti khunji diner seshe.
Sethay premer charam sadhan, jay khase tar sakal bandhan—
Mor hridaypakhir gagan tomar-hridaydese.
Ogo, jani amar sranta diner sakal dhara
Tomar gabheer rater santimajhe klantihara.
Amar dehe dharar paras tomar sudhay hala saras—
Amar dhuiari dhan tomar majhe natun bese.

I know in thy love the message of all love mingles.
I seek my salvation in it alone at the day's end.
The greatest meditation of love is there, all its bonds are loosened.
In thy heart is the sky of the bird in my heart.
O dear, know I that all the streams of my tired days
Become tireless in the bliss of thy dense-deep night.
The touch of the earth in my body has become lively with thy drink.
The very wealth of my dust adores within thee in a new pattern.

Pratidin taba gatha gaba ami sumadhur—
Tumi deho more katha, tumi deho more sur—
Tumi yadi thako mane bikacha kamalasane,
Tumi yadi kara pran taba preme paripur.
Tumi sono yadi gan amar samukhe thaki,
Sudha yadi kare dan tomar udar ankhi,
Tumi yadi dukh-'pare rakha kar snehabhare,
Tumi yadi such hate dambha karaha dur.

Everyday shall I sing thy pleasant song—
Give me speech, give me tunes—
If thou dost remain in the mind in the serene lotus seat
If thou dost feel in life with thy love,
If thou dost listen to the song in front of me,
If thou with generous eyes shower the juice as a gift,
If thou dost place thy affectionate hands upon sorrow,
If thou dost drive away pride from happiness.

Eso go nutan jeeban
Eso go kathor nithur neerab, eso go bheeshan sobha.
Eso apriya biras tikta, eso go asrusalilasikta,
Eso go bhushanabiheen rikta, eso chittapaban.
Thak beenabenu, malateemalika purnimanisi, mayakuhelika—
Eso go prakhar homanalsikha hridayasonitaprasan.
Eso go paramaduhkhanilay, asa-ankur karaha bilay—
Eso sangram, eso mahajoy, eso go maranasadhan.

O come, new life.
O come, hard cruel silent, O come, terribly graceful.
Come, unloving humourless sour, O come, drenched in tears
O come, sans ornaments bare, O come, hilarious to the mind.
Let the *veena* and the flute remain, the malati garland, the full moon-night, the illusory mirage—
O come, the strong flame of the fire of havan, the gobbler of the heart's blood.
O come, the repository of grand sorrow, destroy the germination of the seeds of hope.
Come struggle, come the great victory.
O come, the perpetrator of death.

Khule de taranee, khule de tora, srot bahe yay ye.
Manda manda angabhange nachichhe taranga range—ei bela khule de.
Bhangiye felechhi hal, batase purechhe pal,
Srotamukhe pran man yak bhese yak
Ye yabi amar sathe ei bela ay re.

Unfasten the boat, unfasten, O the current flows on,
With gentle movement of limbs, the waves are dancing in joy—unfasten right now.
The oars have I broken, the sail is swollen in the wind
Let the mind and the heart float away in the mouth of the current
O the one willing to accompany me, come right now.

Ekbar tora ma baliya dak jagatajaner sraban judak,
Himadripashan kende gale yak—mukh tule aji chaho re.
Danda dekhi tora atmapar bhuli, hridaye hridaye chhutuk bijuli—
Prabhatagagane koti sir tuli nirbhaye aji gaho re.
Bis koti kanthe ma bale dakile romancha uthibe ananta nikhile,
Bis koti chhele mayere gherile das dik sukhe hasibe.
Sedin prabhate nutan tapan nutan jeeban karibe bapan
E nahe kahinee, e nahe swapan—asibe se din asibe.
Apanar maye ma bale dakile, apanar bhaye hriday rakhile,
Sab pap tap dure yay chale punya premer batase.
Sethay biraje deb-aseerbad—na thake kalaha na thake bishad—
Ghuche apaman jege othe pran—bimal pratibha bikase.

Call on the mother once, let the ears of the people of the world be appeased,

Let the icy stone melt in weeping—O raise the countenance and behold.

Forgetting the self from others, just stand up, let lightning spark from heart to heart,

Raising millions of heads in the morning sky, O sing sans fear today.

If the call of the mother comes out from two hundred million sons, the endless universe would be thrilled,

If two hundred million sons encircle the mother, every side would happily laugh.

On that day the new sun in the morning would sow new life.

It is neither a story nor is it a dream—that day would certainly come.

In calling one's mother as one's own, endearing one's brother in one's heart,

All sins and repentance run away with the wind of virtuous love.

The blessings of gods pervade there—neither quarrels nor glooms remain—

Disgrace is warded off, life wakes up—pure talent effulges.

Barsha gela, britha gela, kichhui kari ni hay––
Apan sunyata laye jeeban bahiya yay.
Tabu to amar kachhe naba rabi udiyachhe,
Tabu to jeeban dhali bahichhe nabeen bay.
Bahichhe bimal usha tomar asisabanee,
Tomar karunasudha hridaye ditechhe ani.
Rekhechha jagatapure, more to fela ni dure,
Aseem aswase tai pulake sihare kay.

The year waned, in vain it ended, alas, nothing I did!
Life flows on with its own void.
Yet the new sun has set in within me,
Yet the new wind blows over life
The clear dawn carries on your blissful words,
In the heart does it bring forth your juice of *karuna*.
In the abode of the world you have kept me, away did you not throw me.
So with infinite assurance the body is thrilled in joy.

Ihader koro aseerbad.
Dharay uthichhe futi kshudra pranguli, nandaner enechhe sangbad.
Ei hasimukhaguli hasi pachhe yay bhuli,
Pachhe ghere andhar pramad,
Ihader kachhe deke buke rekhe, kole rekhe,
Tomora koro go aseerbad.
Balo, 'sukhe yao chale bhaber taranga dale,
Swarga hate asuk batas—
Sukh duhkha koro hela, se kebal dheukhela
Nachibe tomar charipas.

Bless them.
The little lives have bloomed on earth, the message of the heaven has brought.
These smiling countenances—lest these forget laughter,
Lest darkness engulf in errors—
Calling them close to you, endearing them in the breast and the lap,
O bless them,
Say, 'Depart in happiness amidst the group of waves of the world,
Let the wind come from the heaven—
Neglect all sorrows, that is a mere game of waves
Around you that would dance.'

Ami tomar preme haba sabar kalankabhagee.
Ami sakal dage haba dagi.
Tomar pather kanta karba chayan, yetha tomar dhular sayan.
Setha anchal patba amar— tomar rage anuragee.
Ami suchi-asan tene tene bedaba na bidhan mene,
Ye panke oi charan pade tahari chhap bakshe magi.

With thy love shall I be a sharer of the blemishes of all.
With all scars shall I be marked.
The thorns of thy path where the dust sleeps, shall I pick up.
My dress-ends shall I spread there, devoted am I to your anger.
Pulling the sacred seat on and on, I won't wander in strictures.
I pray for the footprints on the breast, which fall on the mud.

Tomari ichchha hauk purna karunmay swami.
Tomari prem smarane rakhi, charane rakhi asa—
Dao duhkha, dao tap, sakali sahiba ami.
Taba prem-ankhi satata jage, jeneo na jani.
Oi mangalaroop bhuli, tai sokasagare nami.
Anandamay tomar biswa sobhasukhapurna,
Ami apan doshe duhkha pai basana-anugami.
Mohabandha chhinna karo kathin aghate,
Asrusaliladhouta hridye thakho dibasayamee.

Let thy desire be fulfilled, O Lord full of kindness.

Thy love do I keep in remembrance, at thy feet do I submit my aspiration.

Give sorrow, give repentance, all shall I forbear.

Thy love-laced eyes awaken all the time, even knowingly I know not.

That auspicious demeanour do I forget, and so do I plunge into the sea of bereavement.

Joyous is thy universe full of beauty and happiness.

A follower of intentions, I embrace sorrow out of my own fault.

Tear off all shackles of enchantment with rude strokes,

Remain with a heart washed in tears day and night.

Nabajeebaner yatrapathe dao dao ei bar
He hridayeswar—
Premer bitta purna kariya dik chitta;
Yena ei sangsarmajhe taba dakshinamukh raje;
Sukharoope pai taba bhiksha, dukharoope pai taba deeksha;
Man hok kshudratamukta, nikhiler sathe hok yukta,
Subhakarme yena nahi mane klanti
Santi santi santi.

In the journey of new life, bless, bless with this boon,
O Lord of the heart,
Let the wealth of love fill in the mind
As if in this world your positive look adorns.
Your mercy do I receive in the form of happiness, your initiation in that of sorrow.
Let the mind be free from pettiness and be in unison with the world.
Let no boredom be admitted in auspicious work.
Peace, peace, peace.

Base achhi he kabe suniba tomar banee.
Kabe bahir haiba jagate mama jeeban dhanya mani.
Kabe pran jagibe, taba prem gahibe,
Dware dware firi sabar hriday chahibe,
Naranareeman kariya haran charane dibe ani.
Keha sune na gan, jage na pran,
Bifale geet-abasan—
Tomar bachan kariba rachan sadhya nahi nahi.
Tumi na kahile kemane kaba prabal ajeya banee taba,
Tumi ya balibe tai baliba—ami kichhui na jani.
Taba name ami sabare dakiba, hridaye laiba tani.

O seated do I remain when I would listen to thy message!
When I would come out in the world by thanking my life,
When life would wake, thy love would sing,
Trekking from door to door, it would want everyone's heart,
Stealing the minds of men and women, it would place on the feet.
None listens to songs, life does not wake,
In vain the music ends.
That I would compose thy speech is beyond my power.
If thou dost not speak, how would I speak—strong and invincible is thy message.
Whatever do thou speak, I would repeat that—nothing do I know.
In thy name I would call on everyone and clasp in my heart.

Dhay yena mor sakal bhalobasa
Prabhu, tomar pane, tomar pane, tomar pane.
Yay yena mor sakal gabheer asa
Prabhu, tomar kane, tomar kane, tomar kane.
Chitta mama yakhan yethay thake sada yena dey se tomar dake,
Yata bandha sab tute yay yena
Prabhu, tomar tane, tomar tane, tomar tane.
Bahirer ei bhiksha-bhara thali ebar yena nihseshe hay khali,
Antar mor gopane yay bhare
Prabhu, tomar dane, tomar dane, tomar dane.
He bandhu mor, he antaratar, e jeebane ya-kichhu sundar
Sakali aj beje uthuk sure
Prabhu, tomar gane, tomar gane, tomar gane.

All my love as if rushes,
Lord, towards thee, towards thee, towards thee.
All my poignant hope as if reaches,
Lord, thy ears, thy ears, thy ears.
My mind as if responds any time anywhere to thy call
As if all constraints are eliminated,
Lord, with thy attraction, with thy attraction, with thy attraction.
Let this external tray full of alms be fully empty,
Lord, with thy gift, with thy gift, with thy gift.
O my friend, O heart of hearts, whatever is beautiful in this life,
Let all ring up in tunes today,
Lord, with thy song, with thy song, with thy song.

Antara mama bikasita karo antaratara he—
Nirmal karo, ujjwal karo, sundar karo he.
Jagrata karo, udyata karo, nirbhay karo he.
Mangal karo, niralas nihsangsay karo he.
Yukta karo he sabar sange, mukta karo he bandha.
Sanchar karo sakal karma santa tomar chhanda.
Charanapadme mama chita nispandita karo he.
Nandita karo, nandita karo, nandita karo he.

Effulge my heart, O Heart of hearts,
O purify, brighten, and make it beautiful.
O awaken, make responsive and fearless.
O make it good without indolence and doubt.
O unite with all, remove all shackles,
Introduce in all actions thy calm rhythm.
O in the lotus feet make my mind *sans* resonance.
O glorify, glorify, glorify.

Peyechhi abhayapad, ar bhay kare—
Anande chalechhi bhabaparabarapare.
Madhur seetal chhay sok tap dure yay,
Karunakiran tanr arun bikase.
Jeebane marane ar kabhu na chhadiba tanre.

Blessed am I with the feet of the Fearless.
Whom do I fear any more?
Towards the shore of the sea of the world
Am I playing on in joy.
Pleasant and cool is the shadow.
Bereavement and emotion leave apart.
The sun shines His love of compassion.
Never shall I leave Him in life and death any more.

Kena banee taba nahi suni nath he.
Andhajane nayan diye andhakare felile, birahe taba kate dinarat he.
Swapnasama milabe yadi kena go dile chetana—
Chakite sudhu dekha diye chiramaramabedana,
Apan-pane chahi sudhu nayanajalapat he.
Parase taba jeeban naba sahasa yadi jagila,
Kena jeeban bifal kara—maranasaraghat he.
Ahangkar choorna karo, preme man poorna karo,
Hriday man haran kari rakha taba sath he.

Why do I not listen to thy message, O Lord!
By blessing the blind with eyes, thou hast put them in darkness, O in languishment thy days and nights pass!
For an instant the eternal pain of the mind pays a visit only,
O looking at myself, it is only shedding tears!
If all on a sudden new life awoke with thy touch,
Why make it a failure, O a striker of the arrow of death!
Crush pride, fill in the mind with love,
By stealing the heart and the mind, O keep me along with thee!

Tomari sebak karo he aji hate amare.
Chitta-majhe dibarat adesh taba deho nath,
Tomar karma rakho biswaduare.
Karo chhinna mohapas sakal lubdha as,
Lokabhay door kari dao dao.
Rata thako kalyane neerabe nirabhimane,
Magna karo anandarasadhare.

O make me thy servant from today
Give thy orders day and night, O Lord, amidst the mind.
Keep me engaged at thy service at the door of the universe.
Tear off all constraints of passion, all tempting expectation.
Drive, drive away fear from people.
Keep me devoted to goodness in silence and *sans* languishment.
Drown me in the stream of joy.

Oder sathe melao yara charay tomar dhenu,
Tomar name bajay yara benu.
Pashan diye bandha ghate ei-ye kolahaler hate
Kena ami kiser lobhe enu.
Kee dak dake baner pataguli, kar isara-triner anguli!
Pranes amar leelabhare khelen praner khelaghare,
Pakhir mukhe ei-ye khabar penu.

Unite me with them who tend thy cows
Who play on the flute in thy name
On the stone-built bank, in this melee of chaos
Why and for what attraction did I come
What is the call of the forest leaves, whose beckoning is through the grass
The God of my heart does play in the playhouse of the heart with all mysteries.
This is the news that from the mouth of birds did I receive.

Baro asa kare esechhi go, kachhe deke lao,
Firayo na jananee.
Deenaheene keha chahe na, tumi tare rakhibe jani go.
Ar ami-ye kichhu chahi ne, chanatale base thakiba.
Ar ami-ye kichhu chahi ne, jananee bale sudhu dakiba.
Tumi na rakhile, griha ar paiba kotha, kende kende kotha bedaba—
Oi-ye heri tamasaghanaghora gahan rajanee.

O with great hopes have I come, take me aside.
Tell me not to go back, my mother.
Nobody wants the poor and the distressed.
Know I that thou keepest him closer to thee.
No more do I want, at thy feet shall I remain seated.
No more do I want, only shall I call thee as the mother.
Where shall I seek my home *sans* thee, where shall I wander a-weeping!
Yonder do I behold the dense night overcast in deep darkness.

Sabe mili gao re, mili mangalacharo.
Daki laho hridaye priyatame.
Mangal gao anandamane.
Mangal pracharo biswamajhe.

O sing in a chorus, deal with goodness together.
Call on the dearest in the heart.
Sing for goodness in a joyous mind. Disseminate goodness amidst the world.

Tomare jani ne he, tabu man tomate dhay.
Tomare na jene biswa tabu tomate biram pay.
Aseem soundarya taba ke karechhe anubhab he,
Se madhuree chiranaba—
Ami na jene pran sanpechhi tomay.
Tumi jyotir jyoti, ami andha andhare.
Tumi mukta maheeyan, ami magna pathare.
Tumi antaheen, ami kshudra deen—kee apoorba milan tomay amay.

O I know thee not, yet the mind rushes towards thee.
Knowing thee not, the world gets rest in thee.
O who has felt thy endless beauty,
That grace is ever new—
Knowing not, I have submitted my life to thee.
Light of light thou art, in darkness am I blind.
Free and great thou art, in the sea am I immersed.
Endless thou art, a tyro and poor am I—what an exquisite union between thee and me!

Toma lagi nath, jagi jagi he—
Sukh nahi jeebane toma bina.
Sakale chale yay fele chirasaran he—
Tumi kachhe thako sukhe dukhe nath,
Pape tape ar keha nahi.

For thee, Lord, do I awake, awake.
No happiness in life *sans* thee.
O leaving the eternal refuge, everyone departs.
Lord, thou dost remain in happiness and sorrow beside me,
In sin and repentance, none else is there.

Sranta kena ohe pantha, pathaprante base e kee khela.
Aji bahe amritasameeran, chalo chalo eibela.
Tanr dware hero tribhuban danraye,
Setha ananta utsab jage,
Sakal sobha gandha sangeet anander mela.

Why tired, O wayfarer, sitting at the end of the way, what a play!
The pleasant breeze blows today, let's go, go right now.
Behold at His door the three worlds remain standing,
The endless ceremony starts there—
A fair of all beauty, fragrance, music and joy.

Kamana kari ekante
Hauk barashita nikhil biswe sukh santi.
Papatap hingsa sok pasare sakal lok,
Sakal pranee pay kul
Sei taba tapitasaran abhayacharanaprante.

Solemnly do I hope,
Let happiness and peace shower all through the universe.
Let all people leave sin and repentance, hatred and bereavement
Let all living beings get refuge
At the edge of thy shelter for the afflicted, fearless feet.

Nikate dekhiba tomare basana karechhi mane.
Chahiba na he, chahiba na he duradurantar gagane.
Dekhiba tomare grihamajhare jananeesnehe, bhratripreme,
Sata sahasra mangalabandhane.
Heriba utsabamajhe, mangalakaje,
Pratidin heriba jeebane.
Heriba ujjwal bimal moorti taba soke duhkhe marane.
Heriba sajane naranireemukhe, heriba bijane birale he
Gabheer antar-asane.

I have the desire within me that I would encounter thee nearby.
O look shall I not, O towards the distant sky shall I not look.
Inside the room shall I look at thee in the mother's affection, in fraternal love,
In hundreds and thousands of auspicious bonds.
I shall behold amidst the ceremony, in auspicious deeds,
Everyday would I behold in life.
In bereavement, sorrow and death would I behold thy bright and transparent image.
In the countenances of men and women I shall behold with people, O behold shall I in secret and isolation
In the poignant seat of the mind.

Bhay hay pachhe taba name ami amare kari prachar he.

Mohabase pachhe ghire amay taba namagan-ahankar he.

Tomar kachhe kichhu nahi to lukano, antarer katha tumi sab jana—

Ami kata deen, ami kata heen, keha nahi jane ar he.

Kshudra kanthe yabe uthe taba nam biswa sune tomay kare go pranam—

Tai amar pachhe jage abhiman, grase amay andhar he.

Pachhe pratarana kari apanare tomar asane basai amare—

Rakho moha hate, rakho tama hate, rakho rakho barbar he.

O I am afraid lest in thy name do I disseminate myself.

O lest thy name and fame and pride encircle me in enchantment.

Nothing remains secret to thee, the words of the mind are all known to thee—

O nobody else knows how poor and down-trodden I am.

Why thy name arises in the little voice, O listening to that, the world salutes thee—

So lest my languishment arises, O darkness engulfs me,

Lest I deceive myself, make myself seated in thy seat—

O keep me off from enchantment, from darkness, keep, keep time and again!

Dao he hriday bhare dao.
Taranga uthe uthalia sudhasagare,
Sudharase matoara kare dao.
Yei sudharasapane tribhuban mate taha more dao.

Give, O give, filling in the heart.
Waves surge in the sea of drinks.
Intoxicate with the juice of drinks.
Offer me the drink with which the whole world is intoxicated.

Duare base achhi prabhu, sara bela—nayane bahe asrubari.

Sangsare kee achhe he, hriday na pure—

Praner basana prane laye firechhi hetha dware dware.

Sakal feli ami esechhi ekhane, bimukh hoyo na deenaheene—

Ya karo he raba pade.

Lord, at the door am I seated all day long—tears roll on in the eyes—

O what is there in the world, the heart is not fulfilled—

With desires of life I have travelled here from door to door.

Leaving all have I come here, do not ignore the poor and down-trodden—

O whatever you do, I would remain fallen.

E moha-abaran khule dao, dao he.
Sundar mukh taba dekhi nayan bhari,
Chao hridayamajhe chao he.

Open this veil of enchantment, O open!
Let me behold with eyes in fullness thy lovely countenance,
Look amidst the heart, O look!

Aji yata tara taba akase
Sabe mor pran bhari prakase.
Nikhil tomar esechhe chhutiya, mor majhe aji pade tutiya he,
Taba nikunjer manjari yata amari ange bikase.

Dike digante yata ananda labhiyachhe ek gabheer gandha,
Amar chitte milie katre tomar mandire uchhase.
Aji konokhane kareo na jani,
Sunite na pai aji karo banee he,
Nikhil nihswas aji e bakshe bansarir sure bilase.

All the stars in thy firmament tonight,
Filling in my life, effulge.
Thy world has come rushing, O that has today come tearing off to me,
All the flowering buds of thy garden adorn my limbs.

The joy around in the horizon has been blessed with a deep fragrance,
Uniting in my mind together, overflows in thy temple.
None today do I know anywhere,
O nobody's message do I listen today,
In this heart the breath of the world is luxuriously adorned in the tune of the flute.

Saktiroop hero tanr,
Anadita, atandrita,
Bhoorloke bhoobarloke—
Biswakaje, chittamajhe
Dine rate.
Jago re jago jago
Utsahe ullase—
Paran bandho re maranaharan
Paramasakti-sathe.
Sranti alas bishad
Bilas dwidha bibad
Door karo he.
Chalo re—chalo re kalyane,
Chalo re abhaye, chalo re aloke,
Chalo bale.
Dukh sok parihari milo re nikhile
Nikhilanathe.

Behold His image of power,
Joyful, sleepless
On earth and in the heaven—
In the activities of the universe, in the mind
Day and night.
Awake, O awake, awake
In enthusiasm and laughter—
O entwine life with the eliminator of death,
The great power.

Tiredness, indolence, grief,
Luxury, hesitation, conflict—
O drive these away.
O let's go—let's go for goodness,
O let's go fearlessly, O let's go in the light,
Saying, 'Let's go'.
Giving up sorrow and bereavement, O congregate in the universe
With the Lord of the universe.

Maranasagarapare tomra amar,
Tomader smari.
Nikhile rachiya gele apanari ghar,
Tomader smari.
Sangsare jwele gele ye naba alok
Joy hok, joy hok, tari joy hok—
Tomader smari.
Bandeere diye gechha muktir sudha,
Tomader smari. .
Satyer baramale sajale basudha,
Tomader smari.
Rekhe gele banee se ye abhay asok
Tomader smari.
Joy hok, joy hok, tari joy hok—
Tomader smari.

On the shore of the sea of death, you are deathless,
We remember you.
In the world you have built your own abode,
We remember you.
The new light that you have trimmed in the world,
Let victory, victory, victory to that very one—
We remember you.
To the prisoners you have given away the juice of freedom.
We remember you.

With the blessed garland of truth you have adorned the earth.

We remember you.

You have left the message fearless and *sans* bereavement,

Let victory, victory, victory to that very one—

We remember you.

Apan ganer tane, amar
Bandhan yak tute.
Ruddhabaneer andhakare
Kandan jege uthe.
Biswakabir chittamajhe
Bhubanbeena yethay baje
Jeeban tomar surer dharay
Paduk sethay lute.

Chhanda tomar khanda haye
Dwandwa badhay prane.
Antare ar bahire tai
Tan mele na tane.
Sur-hara pran bisham badha,
Sei to andhi, sei to dhandha,
Gan-bhola tui gan fire ne
Yak se apad chhute.

In the pull of my own song,
Let strings be cut off.
In the darkness of barred message,
Weeping is surged up.
Amid the mind of the world poet
Where the *veena* of the world plays on,
Let your life submit there in the flow of tunes.

Your rhymes in divisions

Invite conflicts in life.
So in between the heart and outside,
The tunes differ.
Life *sans* tunes is a great constraint—
The same darkness, the same mystery,
Take back the song, the song-forgetter—
Let that constraint be let off.

Bhalogaiar sesh ye na pai
Prahar hala sesh.
Bhuban jude raila lege
Ananda abes.
Dinanter ei ek konate
Sandhyamegher sesh sonate
Mon ye amar gunjarichhe
Kothay niruddes.

Sayataner klanta fuler
Gandha haoyar 'pare
Angabiheen alingane
Sakal anga bhare.
Ei godhulir dhusarimay
Syamal dharar seemay seemay
Suni bane banantare
Aseem ganer res.

No end of likings do I find out,
Hours waned away.
Throughout the world,
The aura of joy pervaded.
In this corner of the day's end
With the last golden hue,
My mind is humming for
The lost I know not where.

The fragrance of the tired flowers of the evening
Spreads in the wind.
With the clasp of armless arms,
The whole body is adorned.
In the dust of this dusk,
In every end of the green earth,
I listen from forest to forest
The leaving tunes of the endless song.

He mahajeeban, he mahamaran,
Lainu saran, lainu saran.
Andhar pradeepe jwalao sikha,
Parao, parao jyotir tika,
Karo he amar lajjaharan.

Paras ratan tomar charan
Lainu saran, lainu saran.
Ya-kichhu malin, ya-kichhu kalo,
Ya-kichhu birup hok ta bhalo,
Ghuchao ghuchao sab abaran.

O great life, O great death,
I take refuge, I take refuge.
Enkindle the flame of the lamp in darkness,
Put on, put on the mark of effulgence,
O take away my bashfulness.

Thy feet are jewels by touch—
I take refuge, I take refuge.
Whatever is dirty, whatever is black,
Whatever is ugly—let all be good,
Remove, remove all veils.

Bandhan chhendarsadhan habe,
Chhede yaba teer mabhai rabe.
Yanhar hater bijayamala
Rudradaher bahni jwala;
Nami nami se bhairabe.
Kal samudre alor yatri
Sunye ye dhay dibasaratri.
Dak ela tar tarangeri,
Bakshe bajuk bajrabheri
Akul praner se utsabe.

To cut off strings would be the meditation,
With the saying 'Fear not', I would depart.
In whose hands the garland of victory adorns
With the flame of furious burnings,
I salute, I salute, I salute the Furious.
In the sea of time, the traveller of light
Simply rushes towards the endless day and night.
The beckoning came from its very waves.
Let the thunderous bugle play on in the breast
In the ceremony of life *sans* shores.

Aloker pathe prabhu, dao dwar khule—
Alok-piyasi yara achhe ankhi tule,
Pradosher chhayatale harayechhe disa,
Samukhe asichhe ghire nirasar nisa.
Nikhil bhubane taba yara atmahara
Andharer abarane khonje dhrubatara,
Tahader dristi ano rooper jagate—
Aloker pathe.

Towards the path of light, Lord, open the door—
Those thirsty for light remain with eyes raised,
Under the shade of dawn have lost direction,
In front, the night of disappointment is encircling.
In thy universe those who are beside themselves in joy
Seek the pole star in the cover of darkness.
Bring forth their sight in the world of beauty—
In the path of light.

Samukhe santiparabar—
Bhasao taranee he karnadhar.
Tumi habe chirasathi, lao lao he krod pati—
Aseemer pathe jwalibe jyoti dhrubatarakar.
Muktidata, tomar kshama tomar daya
Habe chirapatheya chirayatrar.
Hay yena martyer bandhanakshay, birat biswa bahu meli lay—
Pay antare nirbhay parichay maha-ajanar.

In front is the sea of peace—
Set the boat a-floating, O leader.
Thou wouldst be the eternal comrade, O take, take by placing the lap—
Towards the endless the lustre of the polestar would effulge.
O giver of deliverance, thy forgiveness, thy kindness would be
The eternal treasure for the path of the eternal journey.
Let there be detachment from the earth, the vast universe remains with extending arms,
Let it receive in the heart the fearless identity of the great unknown.

Aji megh kete gechhe sakalbelay,
Eso eso eso hasimukhe—
Eso amar alas diner khelay.
Swapna yata jamechhila asa-nirasay
Tarun praner bifal bhalobasay
Diba akul-pane bhasaye bhantar ganger bhelay.
Duhkhasukher bandhan tari granthi diba khule,
Aji kshanek-tare mora raba apan bhule.
Ye gan hay ni gaoya ye dan hay ni paoya—
Aji purab haoyay tari paritap
Udaba abahelay.

Today the cloud is cleared in the morning.
Come, come, come in the smiling countenance.
Come in the play of my idle days.
The dreams accumulated in hopes and disappointments
In the raft of the ebb-tide river would I float away towards the endless bank.
I would unfasten the knot of sorrow and happiness—
Today, forgetting the self, we would remain for a moment
The song unsung, the gift not received—
The repentance for these would I in the eastern wind
Make a-flying in negligence.

Aji tomay abar chai sunabare
Ye katha sunayechhi bare bare.
Amar parane aji je banee uthichhe baji
Abiram barshanadhare.
Karan sudhayo na, artha nahi tar,
Surer sangket jage punjita bedanar.
Swapne ye banee mane mane dhwaniya uthe kshane kshane
Kane kane gunjariba tai
Badaler andhakare.

Today I would once again want to make you listen
The words that time and again I have made you do.
The message that has rung up in my heart today
In restless shower of rains,
No reason do you ask, it has no meaning,
The signal of accumulated pains of tunes surges.
The message that in the dream sounds up in the mind at times,
That I would muse in ears in the darkness of rains.

Ami kee gan gaba ye bhebe na pai—
Meghla akase utala batase khunje bedai.
Baner gachhe gachhe jegechhe bhasha bhashahara nache-
Mon oder kachhe chanchalatar ragini yache
Saradin biramaheen firi ye tai.
Amar ange suratarange dekechhe ban,
Raser plabane dubiya yai.
Kee katha rayechhe amar maner chhayate
Swapnapradoshe—ami tare ye chai.

What song I would sing I fail to think,
In the cloudy sky I wander seeking in the overflowing wind.
In the trees of the forest language has come up in the speechless dance—
The mind prays for the tune of restlessness to them,
So the whole day do I restlessly wander.
In my limbs the tide has surged in the waves of tunes—
I am drowned in the flood of juice.
What words are stored there in the shade of my mind
At the dawn of dreams—I frantically want her.

Dhako re mukh, chandrama, jalade.

Bihagera thamo thamo. Andhare kando go tumi dhara.

Gabe yadi gao re sabe gao re sata asani-mahaninade—

Bheeshan pralayasangeete jagao jagao, jagao re e bharate.

Banabihanga, tumi o sukhageeti geyo na. Pramodamadira dhali prane prane

Anadaraginee aji kena bajichhe eta harashe—

Chhinde fel beena aji bishader dine.

O cover up the countenances, the moon, the cloud.

Birds, stop, stop. O earth, cry in darkness.

O if you want to sing, sing all, sing in a hundred great sounds of lightning.

Awake, awake in the tremendous song of deluge, O awake in this India.

The forest bird, sing not that song of happiness. Pouring the wine of entertainment,

Why is the tune of joy ringing today with so much gladness?

Tear off the *veena* on this day of sorrow today.

Ek sutre bandhiyachhi sahasrati man,
Ek karye sanpiyachhi sahasra jeeban—
Bande mataram.
Asuk sahasra badha, badhuk parlay,
Amra sahasra pran rahiba nirbhay—
Bande mataram.
Amra daraiba na jhatika-jhanjhay,
Ayut taranga bakshe sahiba helay.
Tute to tutuk ei naswar jeeban,
Tabu na chhindibe kabhu e drida bandhan—
Bande mataram.

In a single thread we have tied up a thousand minds,
To a single activity we have dedicated a thousand lives—
Hail to the mother.
Let a thousand constraints come, let the deluge surge,
We, the thousand lives, would remain fearless—
Hail to the mother.
Afraid we would not be in thunder and storm,
With millions of waves on the breast, we would easily tolerate.
If this mortal body terminates, let it come to an end,
Yet this firm thread would never be torn—
Hail to the mother.

Bendhechha premer pase ohe premamay.
Taba prem lagi dibanisi jagi byakulahriday.
Taba preme kusum hase, taba preme chand bikase,
Premahasi taba usha naba naba,
Prem-nimagan nikhil, niraba,
Taba prem-tare fire ha ha kare udasee malay.
Akul pran mama firibe na sangsare,
Bhulechhe tomari rupe nayan amari.
Jale sthale gaganatale taba sudhabanee satata uthale—
Suniya paran santi na mane,
Akul hriday khonje biswamay o prem-alay.

O Lord of love, thou hast tied me with the strings of love.
With the restless heart, I awake day night for thy love.
With thy love flowers laugh, with thy love the moon effulges,
Thy smile of love is dawn new and new,
The universe immersed in love is silent,
For thy love the aimless wind mournfully blows.
My restless heart will not return to the day-to-day life,
With thy beauty my eyes have been enchanted.
In land and water under the sky thy sweet message always overflows—
Hearing that life is not pacified,
The pining heart seeks that resort of love throughout the world.

Pitar duyare dandaiya sabe bhule yao abhiman.
Eso bhai, eso prane prane aji rekho na re bybadhan.
Sangsare dhula dhuye fele eso, mukhe laye eso hasi.
Hridayer thale laye eso bhai, premafool rasi rasi.
Neeras hridaye apana laiye rahile tanhare bhule
Anath janer mukhapane aha, chahile na mukh tule!
Kathor aghate bytha pele kata, bythile pare pran—
Tuchchha katha niye bibade matiye diba hala abasan.
Tanr kachhe ese tabuo ki aji apanare bhulibe na.
Hridayamajhare deke nite tanre hriday ki khulibe na.
Laiba bantiya sakale miliya premer amrita tanri—
Pitar aseem dhanaratuner sakalei adhikariee.

Standing at the door of Father, forget all anguish.
Come, brother, come, O make no distance between heart and heart.
Wash off the dust of worldly life, bring forth laughter in the countenance.
In the tray of the heart, brother, bring heaps of the flowers of love.
With a dry heart and the self, you have remained by forgetting Him—
Alas, towards the face of the destitute, you did not cast your look!
What a pain you felt in violent shock, made others' hearts aching!
Being engrossed in quarrels out of trifling words, the day ended.

Yet would you not come to Him today and forget yourself,

To call on Him in the heart, would you not disclose it?

It is His nectar of love that all of us would share together—

Everyone has the right to have the infinite treasures and gems of Father.

Dukher bese esechha bale tomare nahi dariba he.
Yekhane bytha tomare setha nibid kare dhariba he.
Andhare mukh dhakile swami, tomare tabu chiniba ami—
Maranarupe asile prabhu, charan dhari mariba he.
Yeman kare dao-na dekha tomare nahi dariba he.
Nayane aji jharichhe jal, jharuk jal nayane he.
Bajichhe buke bajuk taba kathin bahu-bandhane he.
Tumi ye achha bakshe dhare bedana taha janak more—
Chaba na kichhu, kaba na katha, chahiya raba badane.

O though thou hast come in the guise of sorrow, I would not be afraid,
O where pain aches, there I would catch hold of thee closely!
Lord, in darkness thou hast covered the face, yet I would recognise thee—
Lord, if thou comest in the form of death, O holding thy feet, I would die,
O in whatever way thou dost appear, I would not be afraid of thee!
Tears are rolling down from eyes today, O let tears roll down.
O let pain ache in the breast in thy strong bond of strings!
That holding in the breast thou dost remain, let pain inform me of that—
Nothing do I want, not a word would I say, O I would stare at the face!

Buk bendhe tui danda dekhi, bare bare helis ne bhai!
Sudhu tui bhebe bhebei hater lakshmi thelis ne bhai.
Ekta kichhu kare ne thik, bhese fera marar adhik—
Barek e dik barek o dik, e khela ar khelis ne bhai.
Mele ki na mele ratan karte tabu habe yatan—
Na yadi hay maner matan chokher jalta felis ne bhai!
Bhasate hay bhasa bhela, karis ne ar helafela—
Periye yakhan yabe bela takhn ankhi melis ne bhai.

Just stand with firm resolution, do not lean, brother.
Brother, push not the immediate lady luck by simply toying with thoughts.
Decide anything whatsoever, to roam afloating is more than death.
For once this way and next the other—no more play this game, brother.
The gem may be available or not, yet care will have to be ensured—
If it is not up to the mind, shed no tears, brother!
If needed, float the raft, do not neglect or belittle—
When hours would wane, do not open the eyes, brother.

Ami bhay karba na bhay karba na.
Du bela marar age marba na bhai, marba na.
Tareekhana baite gele majhe majhe tufan mele—
Tai bale hal chhede diye kannakati dharba na.
Sakta ya tai sadhte habe, matha tule raiba bhabe—
Sahaj pathe chalba bhebe panker 'pare padba na.
Dharma amar mathay rekhe chalba sidhe rasta dekhe—
Bipad yadi ese pade gharer kone sarba na.

Fear shall I not, I shall not fear.
Prior to dying by day or at night, die shall I not, brother, I shall not die.
To ply the boat, storms at times are encountered.
As such, leaving the oars, scream shall I not.
What is hard is to be strived; with head held high, I shall remain on earth.
Thinking that I shall tread on in the easy way, I shall not fall in the mire.
Keeping religion on the head, I shall tread on the straight path—
If danger befalls, in the corner of the room I shall not move.

Ami hethay thaki sudhu gaite tomar gan,
Diyo tomar jagat-sabhay eituku mor sthan.
Ami tomar bhuban-majhe lagi ni ath kono kaje—
Sudhu kebal sure baje akajer ei pran.
Nisar neerab debalaye tomar aradhan,
Takhan more adesh koro gaite he rajan.
Bhore yakhan akas jude bajbe beena sonar sure
Ami yena na rai dure ei diyo mor maan.

Here do I remain only to sing thy song,
In thy world assembly, give me this much space.
Lord, in thy world I had not been of use to any assignment.
Only this life of inactivity rings in tunes.
In the silent abode of gods at night, thy worship takes place,
O King, order me to sing at that time.
When in the golden tune the *veena* would play on at dawn throughout the sky,
Let me not remain away—extend this honour to me.

Dao he amar bhay bhenge dao.
Amar dike o mukh firao.
Pase theke chinte nari, kon dike ye kee nehari,
Tumi amar hridbiharee hriday-pane hasiya chao.
Bolo amay bolo katha, gaye amar paras karo.
Dakshin hat badiye diye amay tumi tule dharo.
Ya bujhi sab bhul bujhi he, ya khunji sab bhul khunji he—
Hasi michhe, kanna michhe—samne ese e bhul ghuchao.

Remove, remove my fear.
Cast that countenance towards me.
Remaining beside, I fail to recognise, I know not what and in which direction I encounter,
Thou art my heart-farer, look at the heart with a smile.
Tell, tell me, touch my body.
Extending the right hand, hold me up.
Whatever I understand is fully erroneous, O whatever I seek is all wrong.
Laughter is false, false weeping—remove this error by coming near.

Subha karmapathe dharo nirbhay gaan.
Sab durbal sangsay hok abasan.
Chirasaktir nirjhar nitya jhare
Laho se abhishek lalat-pare.
Taba jagrata nirmal nutan pran
Tyagabrate nik deeksha,
Bighna hate nik siksha—
Nishthur sankat dik samman.
Duhkhai hok taba bitta mahan.
Chalo yatri, chalo dinaratri—
Karo amritalokapath anusandhan.
Jadatatamas hao utteerna,
Klantijal karo deernabideerna—
Din-ante aparajita chitte
Mrityutaran teerthe karo snan.

Start fearless songs in the auspicious work.
Let there be an end to all feeble fear.
The fountain of eternal power regularly falls—
Accept that symbol on the forehead.
Let your awakened, pure and new life
Take initiation in the worship of sacrifice,
Let it receive lessons from constraints,
Let cruel adversity offer dignity.
Let sorrow alone be your great treasure.
Tread, traveller, tread day and night—
Investigate the path to the heaven.
Be above the darkness of dullness,
Tear off the veil of boredom.
At the day's end, in unfailing mind,
Bathe in the pilgrimage of crossing the bar.

Jananee, tomar karun charanakhani
Herinu aji e arunakiranaroope.
Jananee, tomar maranaharana banee
Neerab gagane bhariuthe chupe chupe.
Tamare nami he sakal bhubanamajhe,
Tomare nami he sakal jeebanakaje,
Tanu man dhan kari nibedan aji
Bhaktipaban tomar poojar dhoope.
Jananee, tomar karun charanakhani
Herinu aji e arunakiranaroope.

Mother, thy piteous feet
In this sunshine do I behold today.
Mother, thy message of great death
Stealthily fills up in the silent sky.
O I salute thee amidst the whole world,
O I salute thee amidst all acts of life,
Today I submit body, mind and wealth
In the incense of the worship of thee, the fire of devotion.
Mother, thy piteous feet
In this sunshine do I behold today.

Katabar bhebechhinu apana bhuliya
Tomar charane diba hriday khuliya.
Charane dhariya taba kahiba prakasi
Gopane tomare sakha, kata bhalobasi.
Bhechhinu kotha tumi swarger debata,
Kemane tomare kaba pranayer katha.
Bhebechhinu mane mane dure dure thaki
Chirajanma sangopane pujiba ekakee—
Keha janibe na mor gabheer pranay,
Keha dekhibe na mor asrubarichay.
Apani ajike yabe sudhaichha asi,
Kemane prakasi kaba kata bhalobasi.

Many a time did I think that forgetting myself
I would open out my heart at thy feet.
Holding thy feet I would express
How I love thee, friend, in secret.
I thought where thou art, the god of heaven,
How I would tell you the words of love.
Leaving far away, I thought aside,
Throughout life, I would alone worship in secret.
Nobody would know about my profound love,
Nobody would see my tears.
Coming today, when thou art asking me,
How I would express my poignancy of love!

Ekhan ar deri nay dhar go tora hate hate dhar go.
Aj apan pathe firte habe samne milan-swarga.
Ore oi uthechhe sankha beje, khulla duar mandire ye—
Lagna baye yay pachhe, bhai, kothay poojar arghya.
Ekhan yar ya-kichhu ghare saja poojar thalar- 'pare,
Atmadaner utsadharay mangalaghat bhar go.
Aj niteo habe, diteo habe, deri kena karis tabe—
Banchte yadi hay benche ne, marte hay to mar go.

No more delay now, O hold, O hold your hands together.
We would have to return in our own path, ahead is the heaven of unison.
O yonder the conch shell is blown, O the door of the temple is open—
O lest the auspicious moment wanes, brother, where the casket of worship is!
Now decorate in the casket whatever is there to everyone in the room,
O fill in the auspicious pitcher with the originating flow of self-sacrifice.
Today we would have to accept and offer as well, why then do you delay—
O if it is to live, live now, if to die, brave death.

Nisidin bharsa rakhis ore man, habei habe.
Yadi pan kare thakis se pan tomar rabei rabe.
Ore man, habei habe.
Pashansaman achhe pade, pran peye se uthbe nade,
Achhe yara bobar matan tarao katha kabei kabe.
Samay hala, samay hala—ye yar apan bojha tolo;
Duhkha yadi mathay dharis se duhkha tor sabei sabe.
Ghanta yakhan uthbe beje dekhbi sabai asbe seje—
Ek sathe sab yatri yata eki rasta labei labe.

Have assurance day and night, O mind, success would surely be achieved.
If you make a promise, that one would certainly sustain.
O mind, success would surely be achieved.
Befallen like a stone, one, regaining life, would move.
Those who are like the dumb, they, too, would surely speak out.
Time it is, it is time—pick up your burden each,
If you hold sorrow up on the head, that sorrow you would surely tolerate.
When the bell would ring, you would see that everyone dressed would come—
All the travellers together would certainly tread on the same path.

Amra milechhi aj mayer dake.
Gharer haye parer matan bhai chhede bhai kadin thake.
Praner majhe theke theke ay bale oi dekechhe ke,
Sei gabheer sware udas kare—ar ke kare dhare rakhe.
Yethay thaki ye yekhane bandhan achhe prane prane,
Praner tane tene ane—sei praner bedan jane na ke.
Maan apaman gechhe ghuche, nayaner jal gechhe muchhe—
Nabeen ase hriday bhase bhaier pase bhaike dekhe
Kata diner sadhanfale milechhi aj dale dale—
Aj ghare chhele sabai mile dekha diye ay re make.

We have congregated today in the call of the mother
How many days, leaving brothers, the son of the soil like a brother remains!
At intervals amid the heart who is calling yonder, 'Come'!
In that poignant voice making one eccentric who can hold one any more!
Wherever we remain there is a bond from heart to heart
Who knows not the pains of the heart that pulls out of the heart's attraction!
Honour and disgrace have been over, tears have been wiped off—
Seeing the brother beside brothers, the heart flashes in new hopes.
With the results of meditation for days unknown, today we have met in groups—
O the sons of the soil, pay today a visit to the mother together.

Mitila sab kshudha, tanhar premasudha, chalo re ghare laye yai.
Setha ye kata lok peyechhe kata sok, trishita achhe kata bhai.
Dako re tanr name sabare nijadhame, sakale tanr gun gai.
Dukhee katar jane rekho re rekho mane, hridaye sabe deho thain.
Satata chahi tanre bholo re apanare, sabare karo re apan.
Santi aharane, santi bitarane, jeeban karo re yapan.
Eta ye sukh achhe ke taha suniyachhe! chalo re sabare sunai.
Balo re deke balo 'pitar ghare chalo, hethay sokatap nai'.

All hunger is appeased, O let us take home His juice of love.
Many a person has received infinite bereavement there and countless brothers have remained thirsty.
O call on all of them at your own resort in His name, let all of us sing His glory.
O remember the sad and suffered, O give all a refuge in the heart.
O looking at Him all the time forget yourself make all your very own.
O in having and disseminating peace, lead life.
Who has heard that there is so much happiness! O let us make all listen to that.
Tell, O tell by calling all, 'Let's go to the abode of Father, where there is neither bereavement nor repentance'.

Deergha jeebanapath, kata duhkhatap, kata sokadahan—
Geye chali tabu tanr karunar gaan.
Khule rekhechhen tanr amritabhabanadwar—
Sranti ghuchibe, asru muchhibe e pather habe abasan.
Ananter pane chahi anander gaan gahi—
Kshudra sokatap nahi nahi re.
Ananta alay yar kiser bhabana tar—
Nimesher tuchchhabhare haba na re mriyaman.

Long is the sojourn of life, so much sorrow and repentance, so much burning of bereavement –
Yet I go on singing His songs of compassion.
He has kept open the doors of His deathless residence.
Tiredness would be removed, tears would be mopped up, there would be the end of this path.
Looking towards the endless, the songs of joy do I sing—
No, O no petty bereavement or repentance!
One who has unending abode, what thought he has!
O with the insignificant burden of a moment I would not lose heart.

Yakhan tomay aghat kari takhan chini.
Satru haye dandai yakhan, lao ye jini.
E pran yata nijer tare tomari dhan haran kare
Tatai sudhu tomar kachhe hay se rinee.
Ujiye yete chai yatabar garbasukhe
Tomar srorter prabal paras pai ye buke.
Alo yakhan alas-bhare nibiye feli apan ghare
Laksha tara jwalay tomar nisithinee.

When I strike thee, I recognise thee.
When I stand like an enemy, thou becomest victorious.
The more this life steals thy treasure for the self,
The more does it become indebted to thee.
Whenever I want to advance in happiness of pride,
The forceful touch of thy current do I receive in the breast.
When, in idleness, I put off the lamp in my own room,
Thy night enkindles a million stars.

Amra nutan praner char.
Amra thaki pathe ghate, nai amader ghar.
Niye pakka patar punji palabe seet, bhabchha bujhi.
O-sab kede neba, udiye deba dakhin haoar 'par.
Tomay bandhba nutan fuler malay
Basanter ei bandeesalay.
Jeerna jarar chhadmaroope ediye jabe chupe chupe?
Tomar sakal bhooshan dhaka achhe nai ye agochar go.

We are the messengers of new life.
We stay on the way and on the bank, no room do we have.
Are you thinking that with the capital of dry leaves winter would escape?
All those would I snatch away and make those fly in the southern wind.
With the garland of new flowers would I bind thee
In this prison-house of spring.
Wouldst thou stealthily avert in the disguise of the tattered and decayed?
All thy dresses are covered, O this is not beyond our knowledge.

Amra khunji khelar sathee.
Bhor na hatei jagai tader ghumay yara sara rati.
Amra daki pakhir galay, amra nachi bakultalay,
Man bholabar mantra jani, haoyate fand amra pati.
Maranke to mani ne re,
Kaler fansi fansiye diye luth-kara dhan nii ye kede.
Amra tomar manochora, chhadbo na go tomay mora—
Chalechha kon andhar-pane sethao jwale moder bati.

We seek playmates
Prior to dawn we awake those who sleep all night
In the voice of birds we call, we dance under the *vakul* tree,
We know how to forget the mind, in the wind we lay the trap.
O we disobey death,
O by by fastening the noose of time, we snatch away the booty.
We are the thieves of your mind, O we won't release you
To which way of darkness are you proceeding? There, too, our lamp burns.

Amader bhay kahare.
Budo budo chor dakate kee amader karte pare.
Amader rasta soja, naiko gali—naiko jhuli, naiko thali—
Ora ar ya kade kaduk, moder paglami keu kadbe na re.
Amra chai ne aram, chai ne biram,
Chai ne ye fal, chai nne re nam—
Mora othay paday saman nachi,
Saman kheli jite hare.

Of whom are we afraid?
What can the old thieves and robbers do to us?
Our roads are straight— no lanes, no hangers, no bags—
O whatever they seize, they won't seize eccentricities.
Comfort we want not, rest we do not want,
Results we want not, name we do not want,
In ups and downs we equally rejoice,
Equally do we play in win or defeat.

Mora chalba na.
Mukul jhare jharuk, mora falba na.
Suryatara agun bhuge jwale maruk yuge yuge—
Amra yatai pai-na jwala jwalba na.
Baner sakha katha bale, katha jage sagarjale—
Ei bhubane amra kichhui balba na.
Kotha hate lage re tan, jeeban-jale dake re ban—
Amra to ei praner talay talba na.

We won't go on.
Let the buds wither, we won't bear fruit
With burnings of fire let the sun and the stars burn for ages—
Whatever burnings we receive, we won't burn.
The branches of the forest speak, speech awakes in the water of the sea—
Nothing we would say in this world.
O wherefrom the pull comes, O the tide roars in the water of life.
Yet we won't move in this stirring of life.

Dheere bandhu dheere dheere
Chalo tomar bijanamandire.
Jani ne path, nai ye alo, bhitar bahir kaloy kalo,
Tomar charanasabda baran karechhi
Aj ei aranyagabheere.

Dheere bandhu dheere dheere
Chalo andhakarer teere teere.
Chalba mi nisitharate tomar haoyar isarate,
Tomar basanagandha baran karechhi
Aj ei basantasameere.

Slowly, friend, slowly, slowly
Advance towards your lonely temple.
The way I know not, no light is there, deep darkness envelops inside and outside
The sound of your feet have I adorned
In the depth of this forest today.

Slowly, friend, slowly, slowly
Advance towards the banks of darkness.
At midnight would I go on in the signal of your wind,
The fragrance of your dresses have I adored
In the breeze of this spring today.

Ami yabo na go amni chale. Mala tomar deba gale.
Anek sukhe anek dukhe tomar banee nilem buke,
Fagunseshe yabar bela amar banee yaba bale.
Kichhu hala, anek baki. Kshama amay karbe na ki.
Gan esechhe sur ase nai, hala na ye sonano tai—
Se sur amar raila dhaka nayanjale.

O I won't go in that way. Your garland would I put on.
With profuse happiness and sorrow, I have accepted your message in the breast
At the end of the early spring I would deliver my message at the time of departure.
Something is done, many yet to be done. Won't you forgive me?
The song has come but the tune hasn't, O that is why it remains unheard—
That tune of mine has been enveloped in tears.

Bujhi ela, bujhi ela ore pran.
Ebar dhar dekhi tor gan.
Ghase ghase khabar chhote, dhara bujhi siure othe—
Digante oi stabdha akas pete achhe kan.

As if it came, O as if life came.
Begin your song now.
The news runs through the grass, as if the earth shivers—
In the horizon the silent sky yonder is alert in ears.

Ya habar ta habe.
Ye amake kanday se ki amni chhede rabe.
Path hate ye bhuliye ane path ye kothay sei ta jane,
Ghar ye chhaday hat se baday—sei to ghare labe.

What is to take place would happen.
Would the one who makes me weep remain thus, leaving me?
The one who takes away from the path through forgetting alone knows where the path is.
He who makes one leave the room extends hands. Only he welcomes in the room.

Sab kaje hat lagai mora sab kajei.
Badha bandhan nei go nei.
Dekhi khunji bujhi, kebal bhangi gadi yujhi,
Mora sab desetei bedai ghure sab sajei.
Pari naiba pari, nahay jiti kingba hari—
Yadi amnite hal chhadi mari sei lajei.
Apan hater jore amra tuli srijan kare,
Amra pran diye ghar bandhi, thaki tar majhei.

In every work we extend our hands, in every work, of course.
O no constraints or barriers are there.
We see, seek and understand, simply break, build and struggle,
In every country we wander, in all decorations, of course.
We succeed or fail, either win or lose.
Lest we lose heart, we die from that very shame.
With the power of our own hands, we create,
With all our efforts we build houses and reside in these, of course.

Bhayere mor aghat karo bheeshan, he bheeshan.
Kathin kare charan-'pare pranata karo man.
Bendhechhe more nitya kaje pracheere ghera gharer majhe,
Nitya more bendhechhe saje sajer abharan.
Eso he, ohe akasmik, ghiriya felo sakal dik,
Mukta pathe udaye nik nimeshe e jeeban.
Tahar pare parkas hok udar taba sahas chokh—
Taba abhay santimay swaroop puritan.

O Terrible, terribly strike at my fear.
With strong hands make my mind bent at the feet.
In day-to-day regular activities amidst the room encircled in walls
The ornaments for decoration have regularly chained me in dresses.
O come, O the accidental one, encompass all sides,
Let this life be flown away towards the open path in an instant.
Thereafter, let there be an effulgence of thy generous and smiling eyes—
Thy fearless, peaceful own appearance of old.

Ami roope tomay bholaba na, bhalobasay bholaba.
Ami hat diye dwar khulba na go, gan diye dwar kholaba.
Bharaba na bhooshanbhare, sajaba na fuler hare—
Sohag amar mala ka're galay tomar dolaba.
Janbe na keu kon tufane tarangadal nachbe prane,
Chander mato alakh tane joyare dheu tolaba.

In beauty I won't enamour you, in love would I enamour.
O in hands I won't open the door, with songs would I make the door open.
In the burden of ornaments I won't fill in, with the necklace of flowers, I won't decorate,
My loving infatuation would I adorn in a garland and make it swing from your neck.
Nobody would know in which gale the bands of waves would dance in the heart.
Like the moon, in invisible pull I would raise waves in the flow tide.

Ami tomar preme haba sabar kalankabhagee.
Ami sakal dage haba dagi.
Tomar pather kanta karba chayan, yetha tomar dhular sayan.
Setha anchal patba amar—tomar rage anuragee.
Ami suchi-asan tene tene bedaba na bidhan mene,
Ye panke oi charan pade tahari chhap bakshe magi.

With thy love shall I be a sharer of the blemishes of all.
With all scars shall I be marked.
The thorns of thy path where the dust sleeps, shall I pick up.
My dress-ends shall I spread there, devoted am I to thy anger.
Pulling the sacred seat on and on, I won't wander in strictures.
I pray for the footprints on the breast, which fall on the mud.

Jeeban yakhan sukaye yay karunadharay eso.
Sakal madhuree lukaye yay, geetasudharase eso.
Karma yakhan prabal-akar garaji uthiya dhake chari dhar
Hridayaprante he jeebananath, santa charane eso.
Apanare yabe kariya kripan kone pade thake deenaheen man
Duyar khuliya he udar nath, rajasamarohe eso.
Basana yakhan bipul dhulay andha kariya abodhe bhulay,
Ohe pabitra, ohe anidra, rudra aloke eso.

When life is dried up, come in the course of compassion.
All grace is concealed, come in the juice of songs.
When actions in vastness engulf all around in roars,
O Lord of life on the edge of the heart, come in gentle footsteps.
When by making the self miserly, the poor and distressed mind lies in a corner,
O Lord Generous, come in the royal grandeur by opening the door.
When aspirations blind with a sea of dust and makes the senseless forgetful,
O Sacred, O Sleepless, come in furious effulgence.

Nath he, premapathe sab badha bhangiya dao.
Majhe kichhu rekho na, rekho na—
Theko na, theko na doore.
Nirjane sajane antare bahire
Nitya tomare heriba.

O Lord, break all barriers in the way of love.
Keep nothing, nothing amidst.
Do not remain, remain not far.
Alone and in companion, in the heart and outside,
I would always behold thee.

Tumi ebar amay laho he nath, laho.
Ebar tumi firo na he—
Hriday kede niye raho.
Ye din gechhe toma bina tare ar fire chahi na,
Yak se dhulate.
Ekhan tomar alloy jeeban mele yena jagi aharaha.
Kee abese kiser kathay firechhi he yathay tathay
Pathe prantare,
Ebar buker kachhe o mukh rekhe tomar apan banee kaho.
Kata kalush kata fanki ekhano ye achhe baki
Maner gopane,
Amay tar lagi ar firayo na—
Tare agun diye daho.

Accept me now, O Lord, accept.
O do not return this time,
Remain by snatching the heart.
I do not want to get back the day lost sans thee,
Let it go to dust.
Now spreading life in thy light I may always remain awake.
O in what an aroma, in which words have I wandered anywhere and everywhere
In ways and fields!
Now placing thy countenance adjacent to the breast, tell thy own message.
O how much dirt, how much truancy yet remain
In the womb of the mind,
For that do not show me the door,
Burn it with fire.